What is SEO? A Comprehensive Guide for Beginners

RC PRABIR

Published by RC PRABIR, 2024.

WHAT IS SEO? A COMPREHENSIVE GUIDE FOR BEGINNERS

First edition. November 21, 2024.

ISBN: 979-8230300755

Written by RC PRABIR.

Also by RC PRABIR

DIY House Hacks

DIY House Hacks: Clever Fixes for Modern Living

Standalone

Real Ways To Make Money From Home : Proven Offline and Online Strategies for Financial Success

What is SEO? A Comprehensive Guide for Beginners

Table of Contents

What is SEO?

A Comprehensive Guide for Beginners

By

RC Prabir

Why read this book

What it is ? Why it's important ?

In today's digital world, **visibility** is everything. Whether you're a budding entrepreneur, a content creator, or a business owner, standing out in the crowded online space is crucial to your success. The key to achieving this visibility? **SEO**—Search Engine Optimization.

But let's face it: SEO can be intimidating. The jargon, the constantly changing algorithms, the technicalities—it can be overwhelming for anyone just starting out. That's where this book comes in.

"How to Be Viral Online? A Simplified Guide on What Does SEO Mean" is designed to take the mystery out of SEO and make it accessible for everyone. Whether you're looking to **boost your sales, campaign your content, or just increase your online presence**, this guide will help you understand and apply the fundamental principles of SEO in a straightforward, no-nonsense way.

In this book, you won't find complicated theories or convoluted instructions. Instead, I've broken down SEO into simple, actionable steps that you can start using right away. You'll learn how to **optimize your content**, **drive traffic to your website**, and **rank higher on search engines**, all while staying true to what you want to achieve online.

SEO is not just for tech experts or big corporations. It's for anyone who wants to **expand their reach**, **increase their influence**, and make an impact in the digital world. By understanding SEO, you're unlocking the ability to **grow your audience, increase your visibility, and ultimately, go viral online**.

Whether you're a beginner or have dabbled in SEO before, this guide will help you **simplify** and **optimize** your efforts for real, measurable results. So let's dive in and start your journey to going viral online!

IN THIS BOOK-

Learn the essential techniques and strategies of Search Engine Optimization (SEO) with this comprehensive guide for beginners. This book will take you step-by-step through the process of optimizing your website to rank higher in search engine results pages (SERPs) and drive more traffic to your site.

This guide covers everything from keyword research and on-page optimization to off-page optimization and measuring your results. We also provide a variety of tools and resources to help you along the way.

Whether you're a business owner, marketer, or just someone who wants to improve the visibility of their website, this book is for you. Written in an easy-to-understand language, it is designed to make SEO accessible for anyone, regardless of their technical expertise.

With this book, you will learn how to:

- Understand the basics of SEO
- Conduct keyword research
- Optimize your website's on-page and off-page elements
- Measure and analyze your results
- Avoid common SEO mistakes

Don't let the complexity of SEO hold you back from growing your business. Order your copy now and start optimizing your website for search engines like a pro.

Preface

Search Engine Optimization (SEO) is a powerful tool for driving more traffic to your website and growing your business. However, for many people, the world of SEO can be confusing and overwhelming. That's why we wrote this book – to provide a comprehensive guide to SEO for beginners.

In this book, we take a step-by-step approach to explain the basics of SEO and how you can optimize your website to rank higher in search engine results pages (SERPs). We cover everything from keyword research and on-page optimization to off-page optimization and measuring your results. We also provide a variety of tools and resources to help you along the way.

Whether you're a business owner, marketer, or just someone who wants to improve the visibility of their website, this book is for you. Our goal is to make SEO accessible and easy to understand for anyone, regardless of their technical expertise.

We hope that this book will serve as a valuable resource for you as you navigate the world of SEO. We wish you all the best in your SEO journey!

Introduction

Welcome to the world of Search Engine Optimization (SEO). In this book, we will explore the basics of SEO and how you can optimize your website to rank higher in search engine results pages (SERPs). Lets understand first with first 5 basic points -

1: Understanding Search Engine Optimization

BEFORE WE DIVE INTO the technical aspects of SEO, it's important to understand what it is and why it's important. Search engine optimization is the process of improving the visibility and ranking of a website or a web page in search engine results pages (SERPs). This is done by making changes to the website's design, content, and structure to make it more attractive to search engines.

Why is SEO important? With the vast majority of internet traffic being driven by search engines, it's crucial for businesses and individuals to have a website that is optimized for search engines. By appearing at the top of search engine results pages, a website can receive more traffic and ultimately drive more business.

2: Keyword Research

KEYWORD RESEARCH IS the process of identifying the terms and phrases that people are using to search for products, services, or information related to your business. By understanding the language of your target audience, you can create content that is more likely to rank for those keywords.

There are a variety of tools available for keyword research, such as Google Keyword Planner, SEMrush, and Ahrefs. These tools allow you to see how many people are searching for a particular keyword and how difficult it will be to rank for that keyword.

3: On-Page Optimization

ONCE YOU HAVE A LIST of keywords that you want to target, the next step is to optimize your website's on-page elements. This includes things like the title tags, meta descriptions, and header tags. These elements help search engines understand what your website is about and how it should be indexed.

Additionally, it's important to make sure that your website's content is optimized for the keywords you're targeting. This means including the keywords in the body of your content, as well as in the alt tags of any images.

4: Off-Page Optimization

OFF-PAGE OPTIMIZATION refers to the actions you can take outside of your own website to improve its visibility in search engine results pages. One of the most important off-page optimization techniques is link building.

Link building is the process of getting other websites to link back to your site. Search engines view links as "votes" for your website, so the more links you have, the more likely your website is to rank. However, it's important to note that not all links are created equal. High-quality, relevant links from reputable websites will have a much greater impact than low-quality links from spammy sites.

5: Measuring and Analyzing Your Results

THE FINAL STEP IN ANY SEO campaign is to measure and analyze your results. This includes tracking your website's rankings for the keywords you're targeting, as well as monitoring your website's traffic and conversions.

There are a variety of tools available for measuring your SEO results, such as Google Analytics, SEMrush, and Ahrefs. These tools allow you to see how your website is performing in search engine results pages and how your SEO efforts are impacting your bottom line.

Conclusion

SEARCH ENGINE OPTIMIZATION is a long-term process, but with the right strategy and execution, it can be a powerful tool for driving more traffic and business to your website. By understanding the basics of SEO, conducting keyword research, optimizing your website's on-page and off-page elements, and measuring your results, you can create a successful SEO campaign that will help your website stand out in search engine

Getting started in natural referencing (SEO)

Who is this guide for?

If you own content online, manage it, monetize it, or advertise it through Google Search, this guide is for you. It is also for you if you are the owner of a growing business, owner of a dozen sites, natural referencing specialist in a web agency or simple amateur who is interested in SEO and is passionate about the mechanisms of research. If you want a comprehensive overview of SEO basics and our SEO best practices, you've come to the right place. However, this guide will not provide you with a miracle solution so that your site automatically appears first in Google search results. However, we hope that following best practices will allow search engines to crawl,

Search engine optimization (SEO) often consists of making small changes to certain parts of your site. When considered individually, these changes may seem small, but when combined with other optimizations, they can have a noticeable impact on user experience and your site's performance in organic search results. You're probably already familiar with many of the topics covered in this guide, as they're essential ingredients to any web page, but maybe you're not getting the most out of them.

The purpose of a website is to meet user needs, and any optimization should aim to improve their experience. Among these users is a search engine, which helps people discover your content. SEO is all about helping search engines interpret and present content. Your site may be smaller or larger than the one we're using as an example, and may have very different content, but the optimization topics covered in this guide apply to sites of all sizes and types. We hope our guide will give you new ideas to improve your website. Let us know your questions, comments, and stories in the Google Search Central Help Community .

First steps

Glossary

Here is a brief glossary of important terms used in this guide:

- **Index** : Google stores all the web pages it knows about in its *index* . Each index entry describes the content and location (URL) of a page. We talk about *indexing* when Google extracts a page, reads it and adds it to its index: *Google indexed several pages of my site today* .
- **Crawling** : The process of finding new or updated web pages. Google detects URLs in different ways, for example, by following links or reading sitemaps. *Google crawls the web for new pages and then indexes them (if any).*

- **Crawler** : Automated software that crawls (retrieves) web pages and indexes them.
- **Googlebot** : generic name of Google's crawler. *Googlebot constantly crawls the web.*
- **SEO** (natural referencing): process of optimizing websites for search engines. SEO can also refer to a job Are you present on Google?

Determine if your site is in the Google index

SEARCH SITE:FOR THE URL of your site's homepage. If results show up, you're in the index. For example, a search for site:wikipedia.orgreturns these results .

The operator **site:**does not necessarily return all URLs indexed under the prefix specified in the query. Learn more about the operator**site:**

If your site is not on Google

ALTHOUGH BILLIONS OF pages are crawled, it is impossible to take all sites into account. When our crawlers can't find a site, it's usually for one of the following reasons:

- The number of websites with links to your site is insufficient.
- You just put a new site online, and we haven't had time to explore it yet.
- The design of the site does not allow us to properly explore the content.
- We encountered an error while trying to crawl your site.
- Your rules prevent us from crawling the site.

How do I get my site to appear on Google?

GOOGLE IS A FULLY AUTOMATED search engine that uses crawlers to constantly crawl the web and find sites to include in our index. Typically, no action is required on your part other than publishing your site to the web. Most of the sites that appear in our results were not submitted manually, but were detected and added automatically as we crawl the web. Learn more about how Google detects, crawls and serves web pages

Research Essentials outlines the main things to consider when designing a website that meets Google's practices. We can't guarantee that our crawlers will find any particular site, but following the guidelines in Search Essentials helps increase your chances of having your site included in our search results.

The Google Search Console offers tools to help you submit your content to us and monitor your Google search rankings. If you want, Search Console can even send you alerts if we detect critical issues on your site. Sign up for Search Console.

Here are some basic questions to ask yourself about your website when you're just starting out.

- Does my website show up on Google?
- Is the content I offer of good quality?
- Does my local business show up on Google?
- Is my content quickly and easily accessible on all devices?
- Is my website secure?

Do you need an SEO expert?

THE ROLE OF AN EXPERT in SEO (natural referencing) is to improve the visibility of your site in search engines. By following this guide, you will discover how to properly optimize your site. You may also consider hiring a professional to help verify your pages.

Hiring a SEO is an important decision that can help you improve your site and save time. Be sure to study the benefits you can get from it, but also the damage an irresponsible SEO could do to your site. Many SEOs and other agencies and consultants offer useful services to website owners:

- Checking the content or structure of your site
- Technical advice on website development, for example: hosting, redirecting, error pages or the use of JavaScript
- Content development
- Management of online business development campaigns
- Keyword research
- SEO training
- Knowledge of specific markets or regions

Before you start looking for an SEO, we strongly recommend that you familiarize yourself with how search engines work. Your choices as a consumer will be all the more enlightened. We recommend that you review this entire guide and, specifically, the following resources:

- Google 's web crawling, indexing and processing page
- Research Essentials
- How to choose an SEO

If you are considering hiring an SEO, the sooner the better. Redesigning your site or launching a new site is usually the perfect time to recruit one. So you and your SEO can ensure a search engine friendly site is designed from the start. However, an effective SEO can also improve an existing site.

To find out why it is useful to use a SEO and what criteria it is important to take into account in this choice, read the article Do you need a SEO (SEO)? .

Help Google find your content

THE FIRST STEP TO GETTING your site on Google is to make sure we can find it. The best way to do this is to submit a *sitemap* . A sitemap is a file on your site that tells search engines which pages have been added or changed. Learn more about creating and submitting a sitemap

Google also finds pages from links from other pages. Learn how to encourage people to discover your site by promoting it .

Tell us which pages you *don't want* crawled .

Block unwanted crawls using robots . txt (for non-sensitive information)

A ROBOTS.TXT FILE TELLS search engines which parts of your site they can access and therefore crawl. This file, whose name cannot be modified, is placed in the root directory of your site. It is possible that pages blocked by the robots.txt file can still be crawled: for sensitive pages, use a more secure method.

brandonsbaseballcards.com/robots.txt

Tell Google not to crawl any URLs in the shopping cart or images in the icons folder,

because they won't be useful in Google Search results.

User-agent: googlebot

Disallow: /checkout/

Disallow: /icons/

You may not want certain pages that are less relevant to search results to be crawled. Note that if your site uses subdomains and you want certain pages not to be crawled for a particular subdomain, you will need to create a separate robots.txt file for that subdomain. To learn more about robots.txt files, check out this guide on how to use them .

Learn about the different ways to block content from appearing in search results .

To avoid :

- Allow Google to crawl your internal search results pages (people don't like to click on a search result and land on another search results page on your site)
- Allow crawling of URLs created as part of proxy services

Use more secure methods for sensitive information

A ROBOTS.TXT FILE IS not an appropriate or effective way to block sensitive or confidential content. It only tells scrupulous crawlers that the pages aren't intended for them, but it doesn't stop your server from serving those pages to a requesting browser. This is because search engines can still refer to the URLs you are blocking (stating just the URL, no title link or excerpt) if there are links to them somewhere on the internet, for example on your referrer URL log files. Also, non-compliant or malicious search engines that do not recognize the robots exclusion protocol could violate the instructions in your robots.txt file. At last,

If you just don't want the page to show up on Google, use the noindex. Note however that this does not prevent Internet users from accessing this page if they have its link. To ensure real security, use appropriate authorization methods (require a user password, for example) or delete the page entirely from your site.

Help Google (and people) interpret your content

Allow Google to see your page as people see it

WHEN GOOGLEBOT CRAWLS a page, it should see the page the same as any web user . For optimal display and indexing, the JavaScript, CSS, and image files your website uses should always be accessible by Google. If the site's robots.txt file prevents the crawling of these elements, it directly affects the display and indexing of content by our algorithms. Therefore, it is possible that the ranking of the site is not optimal.

Recommended Action : Use the URL Inspection tool . This tool closely replicates the way Google sees and displays your content, and helps you identify and fix a number of indexing issues on your site.

Create unique and accurate page titles

AN ELEMENT <TITLE>TELLS users and search engines what a specific page is about. Place the element <title>in the <head>HTML document tag, then create unique title text for each page on your site.

<html>

<head>

<title>Brandon's Baseball Cards - Buy Cards, Baseball News, Card Prices</title>

<meta name="description" content="Brandon's Baseball Cards provides a large selection of

vintage and modern baseball cards for sale.

We also offer daily baseball news and events.">

</head>

<body>

...

Influencing your title links and snippets in search results

IF YOUR DOCUMENT IS on a search results page, the item's content <title>may show up as a title link for the search result (if you're unfamiliar with the different parts of a Google search result , check out this video on the anatomy of a search result .

<title>Your homepage element can show the name of your website or business and include other important information, such as the physical location of your business, or some information about the domain or services offered.

Accurately describe the content of the page

CHOOSE TITLE TEXT THAT is readable and evocative of the content of the page.

To avoid :

- Using text in the element <title>that has no relation to the content of the page
- Use default or vague titles like "Untitled" or "New Page 1"

<TITLE>**Create unique elements for each page**

Make sure each page on your site has unique text in the element <title>. This will allow Google to differentiate between them. If your site uses separate mobile pages, don't forget to add descriptive text in the elements <title>of the mobile versions.

To avoid :

- Use a single title in all elements <title>of pages on your site or a large number of pages

USE <title>**short but descriptive elements**

Items <title>can be both short and informative. If the item text <title>is too long or deemed less relevant, Google may display only part of the text in the item <title>or automatically generate a title link in the search result.

To avoid :

- Use very long text in elements <title>without providing particularly useful information for Internet users
- Accumulate unnecessary keywords in the element<title>

Use the meta description tag

A PAGE'S META DESCRIPTION tag provides Google and other search engines with a summary of the page. The title of a page consists of a few words or a phrase, while the meta description tag can contain one or two sentences, or even a short paragraph. Like the element <title>, the meta description tag is placed within the element <head>of the HTML document.

```
<html>
<head>
<title>Brandon's Baseball Cards - Buy Cards, Baseball News, Card Prices</title>
<meta name="description" content="Brandon's Baseball Cards provides a large selection of vintage and modern baseball cards for sale. We also offer daily baseball news and events.">
</head>
<body>
...
```

What is the purpose of meta description tags?

META DESCRIPTION TAGS are important because Google might use them as snippets to represent your pages in Google search results. Note that we use the conditional, because Google reserves the right to choose to use a relevant section of the visible text of your page if it corresponds to a request from the Internet user. Adding meta description tags to each of your pages is a good practice in case Google can't find a suitable text selection to use in the snippet. Find out how to create quality meta descriptions .

Accurately summarize the content of the page

WRITE A DESCRIPTION that can inform and engage people who see your meta description tag as a snippet in a search result. There is no maximum or minimum length for the text contained in a meta tag description, but we recommend making it long enough to appear fully in Google search (note that searchers may see snippets of different sizes depending on their search and the device they use), and that it includes all the relevant information so that Internet users know if the page will be useful to them.

To avoid :

- Write a meta description tag unrelated to the content of the page
- Use generic descriptions like "This is a webpage" or "soccer cards page"
- Use only keywords in the description
- Copy and paste the entire content of the document into the meta description tag

Use unique descriptions for each page

A DIFFERENT META DESCRIPTION tag for each page helps searchers and Google, especially in searches where searchers might see multiple pages on your domain (for example, searches using the operatorsite:). If your site has thousands or even millions of pages, it is humanly impossible to manually add meta description tags to each one. We advise you instead, in this case, to generate meta description tags automatically according to the content of each page.

To avoid :

- Use a single meta description tag for all or many of your site's pages

Use title tags to highlight important text

USE RELEVANT HEADINGS to indicate important topics and organize content hierarchically. This will make it easier for users to navigate your document.

Imagine you are writing a plan

AS YOU WOULD WHEN WRITING an outline for a multi-page article, think about what the main and minor points of the page's content will be, and decide where it would make sense to use title tags.

To avoid :

- Placing text in title tags that would not be useful in defining page structure.
- Use title tags where other tags like <em>and <strong>would be more appropriate.
- Choose title tags of different sizes irregularly.

Use headings sparingly on the page

USE TITLE TAGS APPROPRIATELY. Too many title tags on a page can interfere with content viewing and prevent viewers from determining where one topic ends and the next begins.

To avoid :

- Using an excessive number of title tags on a page.
- Use very long titles.
- Use title tags only to format text, not to present structure

Add structured data markup

STRUCTURED DATA IS code you can add to pages on your site to describe your content to search engines, so they can more easily understand what's on your pages. Search engines can use this interpretation to display your content in a useful (and eye-catching) way in search results. This can help you attract the right kind of customers for your business.

Bianchi Specialissima X-4 | The vintage bicycle store
http://www.example.com/vintate-bikes/Bianchi/Specialissima-X-4.html ▾
★★★★★ Rating: 4.9 - 5 reviews - $2700.00
Exclusive to the Vintage Bicycle Store — excellent condition 1980s Bianchi Specialissima X-4. Fully functional, custom engravings, original parts...

For example, if you have an online store and you mark up a specific product page, it will help us to understand that it presents, for example, a bicycle, with its price and customer reviews. We may display this information in the search results snippet for relevant queries. We call this rich results.

Structured data markup allows us not only to generate rich results, but also to serve relevant results in other formats. For example, if you have a brick-and-mortar store, tagging your opening hours helps potential customers find you precisely when they're looking for you, and tells them whether your store is open or closed when they search.

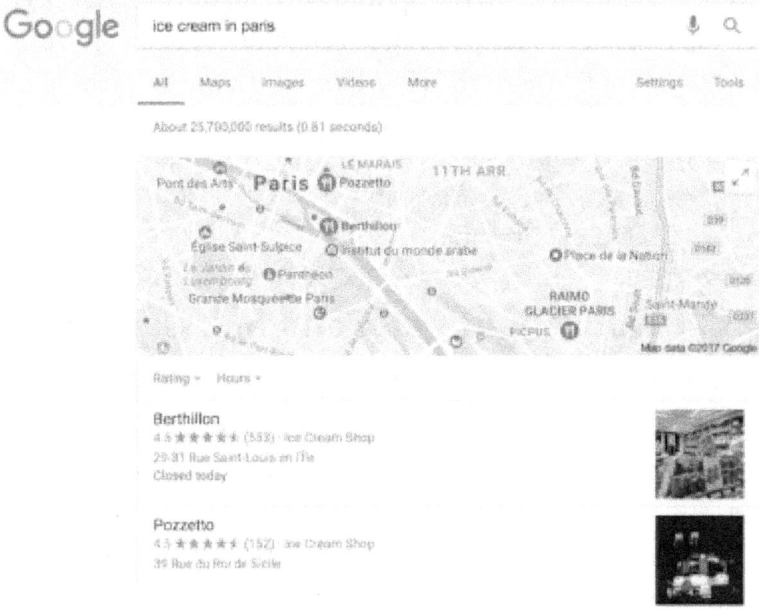

You can tag many business entities:

- The products you sell
- The location of the establishment
- Videos about your products or your company
- Opening hours
- The calendar of events
- Recipes
- Your company logo, and more

WE RECOMMEND THAT YOU use structured data with any of the accepted annotation markup to describe your content. You can add the markup to the HTML of your pages or use tools like the Data Highlighter and Markup Helper Tool .

Check your markup using the rich results test

ONCE YOU'VE MARKED up your content, you can use the Google Rich Results Test to check the implementation for errors. You can enter the content URL or copy the HTML code that includes the markup.

To avoid :

- Use invalid markup

Use Data Highlighter and Markup Helper

IF YOU WANT TO PERFORM structured markup without changing your site's source code, you can use Data Highlighter , a tool built into Search Console and compatible with a subset of content types.

If you want to get the markup code ready to copy and paste onto your page, try the Markup Helper .

To avoid :

- Modify your site's source code when you are unsure of the markup implementation

Track your tagged pages

SEARCH CONSOLE 'S VARIOUS RICH results reports allow you to determine the number of pages on your site where we detected a specific type of markup, the number of times they were shown in search results, and the number of times people clicked on it in the last 90 days. They also indicate the errors that we have detected.

To avoid :

- Add markup data that is not visible to web users

- Create fake reviews or add irrelevant tags

Manage your appearance in Google search results

BY ADDING CORRECT STRUCTURED data to your pages, you make them eligible for many special features in Google search results, for example, review stars, attractive presentation in results and more. Check out the gallery of search result types your page may be eligible for .

Organize the tree of your site

Understand how search engines use URLs

SEARCH ENGINES NEED a unique URL per piece of content to be able to crawl it, index it and redirect users to it. To be displayed correctly in search, content of a different nature (for example, different products in a store) as well as modified content (for example, translations or regional variations) must correspond to distinct URLs.

URLs are usually divided into several distinct sections:

protocol://hostname/path/filename?querystring#fragment

Example :

https://www.example.com/RunningShoes/Womens.htm?size=8#info

Google recommends that all websites use https://where possible. The hostname is where your website is hosted: it's often the same domain name as your emails. Google distinguishes between versions with and without "www" (for example, www.example.comor only example.com). When adding your website to Search Console, we recommend adding both the http://and versions https://, as well as the versions with and without "www".

The path, filename, and query string indicate what content on your server is being accessed. These three elements are case-sensitive, so FILEmay point to a different URL than file. The host name and protocol are not case-sensitive; upper or lower case does not matter.

A fragment (in this case, #info) typically identifies the part of the page the browser is browsing. Since the content itself is generally identical regardless of the fragment, search engines generally ignore the fragments used.

When referring to the homepage, a slash after the hostname is optional, because it points to the same content (https://example.com/ is the same as https://example.com). With respect to path and filename, a trailing slash is considered a different URL (signifying a file or a directory). For example, https://example.com/fishis not the same as https://example.com/fish/.

Importance of navigation for search engines

WEBSITE NAVIGATION is important to help visitors quickly find the content they are looking for. It can also help search engines interpret content that the website owner considers important. Although Google search results are delivered at a page level, Google also likes to get an idea of a page's role in a site as a whole.

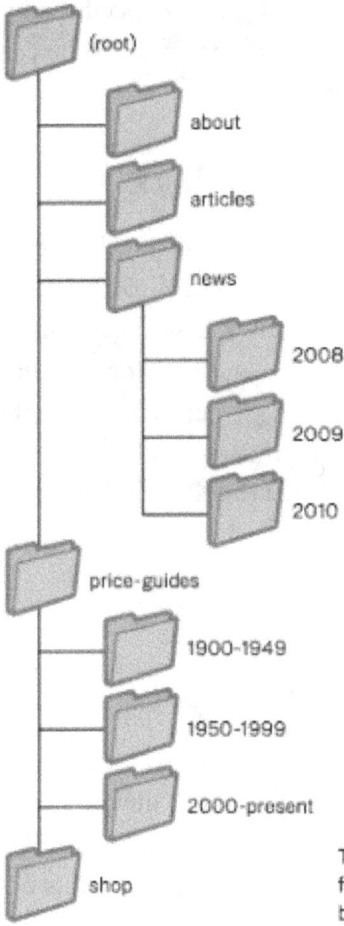

The directory structure for our small website on baseball cards.

Plan your browsing based on your homepage

ALL SITES HAVE A HOME page or root page, which is usually the most visited page of the site and is, for many visitors, the starting point of navigation. Unless your site is only made up of a handful of pages, think about how your visitors will get from a general page (your root page) to a page with more specific content. Do you have enough pages related to a specific subject to create a page describing this related content (eg root page -> list of related topics -> specific subject)? Do you have hundreds of different products that need to be categorized into multiple categories and subcategories?

Use breadcrumb lists

A BREADCRUMB IS A LINE of internal links, at the top or bottom of the page, that allows visitors to quickly return to a previous section or to the root page. In many breadcrumbs, the most general page (often the root page) is the first link on the left, and the more specific sections appear to its right. We recommend using structured data markup in the form of breadcrumbs when displaying this type of content.

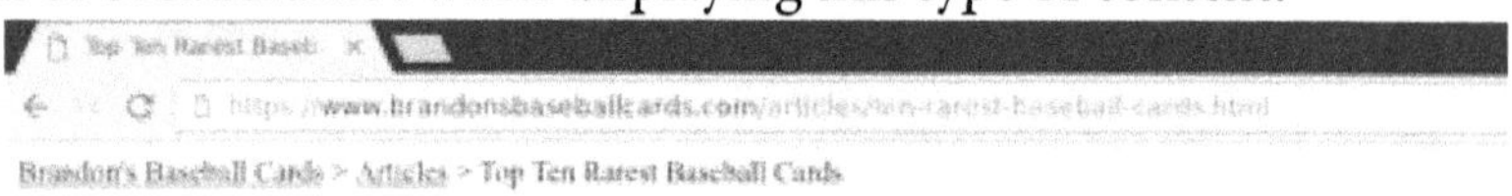

Create a simple navigation page for users

A NAVIGATION PAGE IS a simple page on your site that displays the structure of your site and usually consists of a hierarchical list of site pages. Visitors can refer to this page if they are having trouble finding pages on your site. Although search engines also visit this page to get a broad scope of crawling your site's pages, it is primarily for human visitors.

Create a naturally structured hierarchy

MAKE IT AS EASY AS possible for users to navigate from general content to the more specific content they are looking for on your site. Add navigation pages when it makes sense and integrate them effectively into your internal linking structure. Make sure that all pages on your site are accessible via links and do not require an internal search function. Add links to related pages, if available, to help people discover similar content.

To avoid :

- Create complex webs of navigational links, for example, linking every page on your site to every other page
- Slice your content too much (so it takes twenty clicks to get to the content you want from the homepage)

Use text for navigation

USING TEXT LINKS TO navigate from page to page makes it easier for search engines to crawl and interpret your site. When using JavaScript to create a page, use elements ain attribute values hreffor URLs and generate all menu items on page load instead of waiting for user interaction.

To avoid :

- Have navigation entirely based on images or animations
- Use navigation that requires script-based event handling

Create a navigation page for Internet users and a sitemap for search engines

INCLUDE A SIMPLE NAVIGATION page for your entire site (or the most important pages, if you have hundreds or thousands) for web surfers. Create an XML sitemap file to ensure that search engines discover added and updated pages on your site, listing all relevant URLs along with the last modification dates of their main content.

To avoid :

- Letting your navigation page become stale with non-working links
- Create a navigation page that simply lists the pages without organizing them (by subject, for example)

View helpful 404 error pages

INTERNET USERS SOMETIMES access a page that does not exist on your site either by following a broken link or by typing the wrong URL. A personalized 404 error page that redirects users to a functional page on your site can greatly improve the user experience. Consider including a link to your root page and links to popular or related content on your site. You can use the Google Search Console to find the sources of URLs causing Page Not Found errors .

To avoid :

- Allow your 404 error pages to be indexed in search engines (make sure your web server is configured to generate an HTTP 404 status code or, in the case of JavaScript-based sites, include a tag noindexwhen non-existent pages are requested)
- Block crawling of 404 pages via the robots.txt file
- Provide only a vague message like "Not Found" or "404", or don't provide a 404 page at all
- Use a style inconsistent with the rest of your site for your 404 pages

Simple URLs inform about content

NOT ONLY DOES CREATING descriptive categories and filenames for documents on your website help you better organize your website, it can also create simpler and more user-friendly URLs for people to link to your website. contents. Long or complex URLs with few recognizable words can scare visitors away.

The following URLs can be confusing:

https://www.brandonsbaseballcards.com/folder1/22447478/x2/14032015.html

If your URL is descriptive, it may be more useful and easily understood in various contexts:

https://www.brandonsbaseballcards.com/article/ten-rarest-baseball-cards.html

URLs show up in search results

FINALLY, REMEMBER THAT a document's URL usually appears in a given form in a Google search result, near the document's title.

Google is able to crawl all types of URL structures, even relatively complex ones. However, it's a good idea to spend time simplifying your URLs as much as possible.

Use words in URLs

URLS WITH WORDS RELEVANT to your site's content and structure are more friendly to visitors viewing your site.

To avoid :

- Using long URLs with unnecessary parameters and session IDs
- Choose generic page names likepage1.html
- Using too many keywords likebaseball-cards-baseball-cards-

baseballcards.html

Create a simple directory structure

USE A DIRECTORY STRUCTURE that organizes your content well and lets visitors know where they are on the site. Use this structure to indicate the type of content that can be found on a particular URL.

To avoid :

- Use subdirectory nesting such as.../dir1/dir2/dir3/dir4/dir5/dir6/page.html
- Use directory names that have no relation to the content

Provide a single URL version to access a document

TO PREVENT USERS FROM using multiple versions of the same URL (which could split the reputation of this content between URLs), strive to use and reference only one URL in structure and internal links of your pages. If you find that multiple URLs lead to the same content, consider setting up 301 redirects from the non-preferred URLs to the dominant URL to correct the problem. If you are unable to perform redirects, you can also use the link element rel="canonical".

To avoid :

- Have subdomain and root directory pages that access the same content (eg, domain.com/page.htmland sub.domain.com/page.html)

Optimize your content

Make your site interesting and useful

CREATING ENGAGING AND useful content is likely to have a bigger impact on your website than any of the other factors listed here. Internet users know how to recognize quality content and are likely to redirect other Internet users to it. They may do so through blog posts, social media services, email, forums, or other means.

Natural interest and word of mouth contribute to the reputation of your site both with Internet users and Google, and these distribution methods are often linked to the quality of the content.

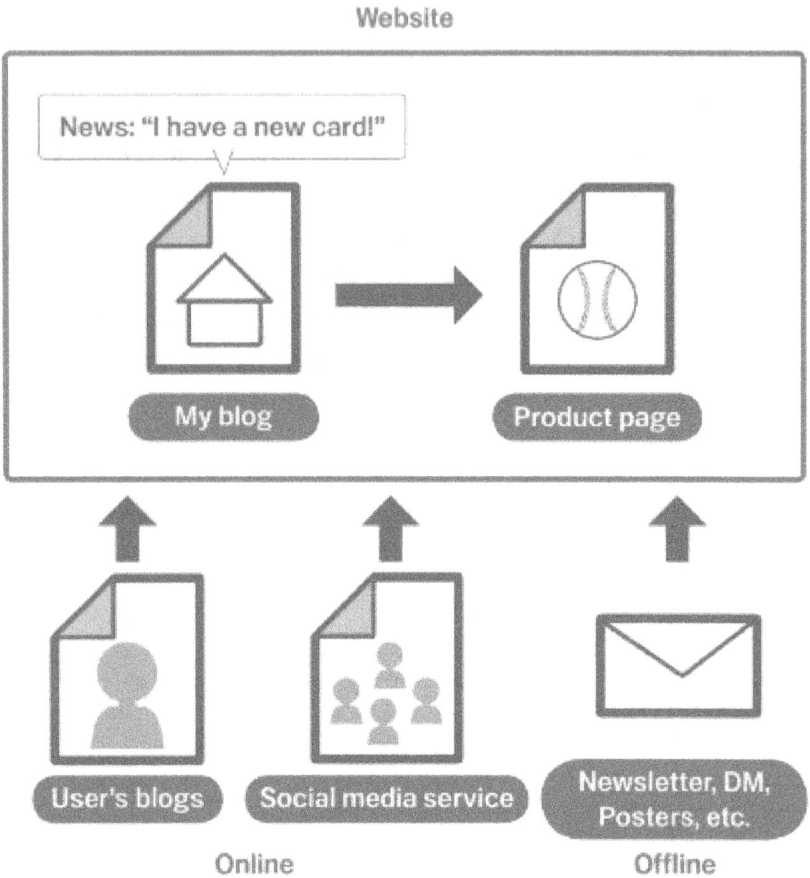

Understand what your readers want (and meet their needs)

THINK ABOUT THE WORDS someone might search for to find some of your content. Internet users who are knowledgeable about the subject of your site may use different keywords than those chosen by novices in their search queries. For example, a long-time football fan might search for "fifa", the acronym for Fédération Internationale de Football Association, while a new fan might use a more general query like "football playoffs". Anticipating these differences in search behaviors and taking them into account when writing your content (using the right mix of phrases) could produce positive results. Google Ads offers a keyword plannerpractice that lets you discover new keyword variations and the approximate search volume for each. The Google Search Console also provides the top search queries for your site and the ones that drove the most people to your site in the Performance report .

Consider creating a useful new service that no other site offers. You could also write an original study, post a hot topic, or leverage your unique user base. Other sites may lack the resources or expertise to do this.

Write easy-to-read text

Internet users appreciate well-written and easy-to-read content.

To avoid :

- Neglecting the writing of a text and leaving grammar and spelling errors
- Use clumsy or poorly written content
- Embed text in images and videos, as people may try to copy and paste it, and search engines won't be able to read it

Organize your topics clearly

IT IS ALWAYS BENEFICIAL to organize your content so visitors know where one topic begins and another ends. Dividing your content into logical blocks or divisions helps people find the information they're looking for more quickly.

To avoid :

- Put large amounts of text dealing with various subjects on the same page, without materializing the separation using paragraphs, subtitles or a page layout

Create original and unique content

ORIGINAL CONTENT WILL keep your existing visitors coming back and attract new ones.

To avoid :

- Repeat (or even copy) existing content that would provide little value to Internet users
- Insert identical or almost identical content in several places on your site.

Optimize content for Internet users , not for search engines

WHEN YOU DESIGN A SITE with the needs of Internet users in mind, while ensuring that the site is easily accessible to search engines, the results are generally positive.

To avoid :

- Insert many useless keywords intended for search engines, which would be boring or nonsense for Internet users
- Use blocks of text like "frequent misspellings used to get to this page", which would add little value for internet users
- Conceal text from Internet users in a deceptive way , but make it accessible to search engines

Act in a way that cultivates user trust

WHEN THEY CONSULT A site, Internet users appreciate it all the more if they feel confident about it.

Sites that have a good reputation create that sense of trust. To build your reputation, it is essential to demonstrate your expertise and consistency in a specific area.

Indicate who publishes your site and provides the content, as well as the purposes they want to meet. If you offer a sales or financial transaction website, be sure to provide accurate information about your customer service . This will help users troubleshoot issues. If you have a news site, make it clear who is responsible for the content.

The use of appropriate technologies is also important. If a marketplace's checkout page doesn't offer a secure connection, customers can't trust it.

Clearly indicate sources

THE QUALITY OF A SITE is proportional to its expertise and reliability. Make sure its content is created or edited by people who know what they are talking about. For example, to help Internet users understand the level of expertise of your articles, it can be useful to indicate your sources. In the predominantly scientific pages, it is also advisable to report proven consensus, where applicable.

Provide an appropriate amount of content for the subject matter

CREATING HIGH-QUALITY content requires a lot of time, effort, expertise or talent/skills, or all of these. The content must faithfully describe the facts, be exhaustive and clearly written. For example, if you're using your page to share a recipe, provide a complete, easy-to-follow recipe, rather than a set of ingredients or a basic description of the dish.

To avoid :

- Provide content that only partially meets the needs of the page

Avoid distracting readers with advertisements

WE UNDERSTAND THAT ads need to be visible. However, they must not distract Internet users or prevent them from reading the content of the site. Please therefore avoid advertisements, content supplements or interstitial pages (pages displayed before or after the expected content) which complicate the use of the website. Learn more about this topic

To avoid :

- Include annoying ads in your pages

Use links wisely

Write appropriate link texts

THE TEXT OF A LINK corresponds to its visible part. It gives Internet users and Google information on the page to which the link points. Links on your page can be internal, meaning redirecting to other pages on your site, or external, meaning leading to content on other sites. In any case, the more relevant your anchor text, the easier it will be for Internet users and for Google to understand what your page is about.

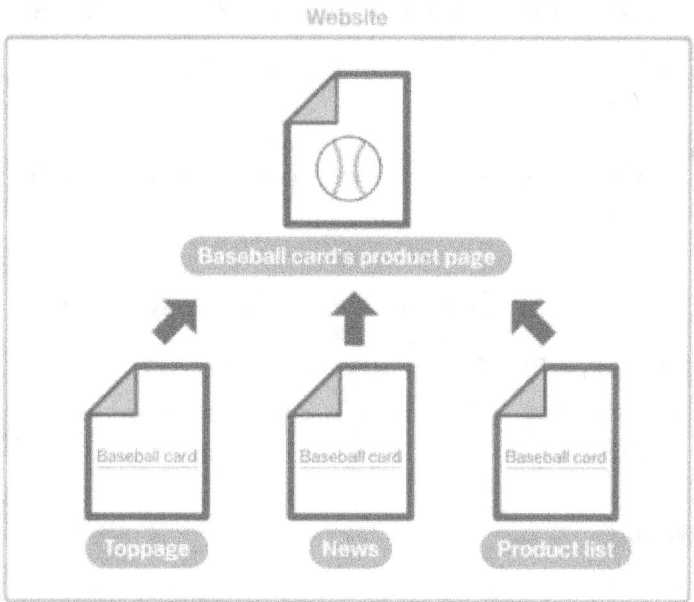

WITH PROPER ANCHOR text, users and search engines can easily interpret what the linked pages contain.

Choose a descriptive text

WRITE ANCHOR TEXT THAT provides at least a general idea of the content of the page.

To avoid :

- Choose generic anchor text like "page", "post" or "click here"
- Use text that is off-topic or unrelated to the content of the linked page
- Use the page URL as anchor text, except in legitimate cases, such as promoting or referencing a new website address

WRITE A CONCISE TEXT

Use a short, but descriptive text, consisting of a few words or a short sentence.

To avoid :

- Write long anchor text, such as a long sentence or short paragraph

Format links for easy identification

HELP PEOPLE TELL THE difference between regular text and the anchor text of your links. Your content becomes less useful if people don't see the links or accidentally click on them.

To avoid :

- Use CSS styling or text that makes links look like regular text

Thinking about anchor text for internal links

LINKS ARE TYPICALLY used to point to external websites, but paying more attention to the anchor text used for internal links can help people and Google better navigate your site.

To avoid :

- Using anchor text that is too long or with too many keywords just for search engines
- Create unnecessary links that do not help users navigate the site

Pay attention to links to other sites

YOUR SITE'S REPUTATION may be passed on to another site you link to. Sometimes people take advantage of this association by adding links to their own site in your comment sections or newsgroups. You may also want to mention a site negatively and not pass on your reputation to them. Imagine, for example, that you are writing a blog post about comment spammers and you want to name a site that recently spammed your blog in the comments. You want to notify other site visitors by including the link in your content. However, you do not want to associate your reputation with this site. It is therefore wise to use the attribute nofollow.

The attribute nofollowcan also be useful when it comes to widget links. If you're using a third-party widget to enhance your site experience and engage people, check to see if it contains links that you didn't intend to put on your site with the widget. Some widgets may add links to your site that go against your team's choice and contain anchor text that you, as the website owner, cannot control. Removing these unwanted links from the widget is not possible, but you can always disable them using the nofollow. If you are creating a widget for the functionality or content you provide, be sure to include the attributenofollowon the links in the default code snippet.

Finally, if you want to unfollow any links from a page, you can add the tag <meta name="robots" content="nofollow">in the <head>page tag. You can find more information about meta tags for robots in our documentation.

Fight spam in comments with the attribute nofollow

TO TELL GOOGLE NOT to follow links on a page, or to have your page's reputation not passed on to related pages, set the value of rela link 's attribute to nofollowor ugc. To unfollow a link, you need to add rel="nofollow"or a more specific attribute likeugc in the link's anchor tag, as shown below:

<a href="https://www.example.com" **rel="nofollow"**>Anchor text here</a>

Where :

<a href="https://www.example.com" **rel="ugc"**>Anchor text here</a>

When to use the "nofollow" attribute? If your site has a blog that has public comments enabled, links in those comments may carry your reputation to pages you don't endorse. Blog comment areas are highly susceptible to spam. By adding the "nofollow" tag to links added by Internet users, you prevent your page's hard-earned reputation from being passed on to spammy sites.

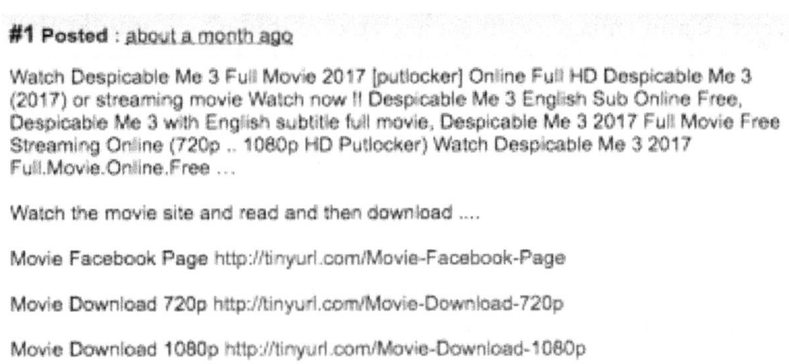
#1 Posted : about a month ago

Watch Despicable Me 3 Full Movie 2017 [putlocker] Online Full HD Despicable Me 3 (2017) or streaming movie Watch now !! Despicable Me 3 English Sub Online Free, Despicable Me 3 with English subtitle full movie, Despicable Me 3 2017 Full Movie Free Streaming Online (720p .. 1080p HD Putlocker) Watch Despicable Me 3 2017 Full.Movie.Online.Free ...

Watch the movie site and read and then download ....

Movie Facebook Page http://tinyurl.com/Movie-Facebook-Page

Movie Download 720p http://tinyurl.com/Movie-Download-720p

Movie Download 1080p http://tinyurl.com/Movie-Download-1080p

Automatically add the attribute nofollow to comment columns and newsgroups

MANY SOFTWARE PACKAGES for blogs automatically add the attribute nofollowto customer reviews, but those that don't benefit from this automatic addition can make this change manually. This advice also applies to other areas of your site that may involve user-generated content, such as visitor logs, forums, bulletin boards, recommendation lists, etc. If you want to vouch for links added by third parties (if a speaker is approved on your site, for example), it is not necessary to usenofollowon the links. On the other hand, links to sites that Google considers to be spammy can affect your own site's reputation. You can find more tips on how to avoid comment spam by using captchas and enabling comment moderation, for example , in the Google Search Central documentation .

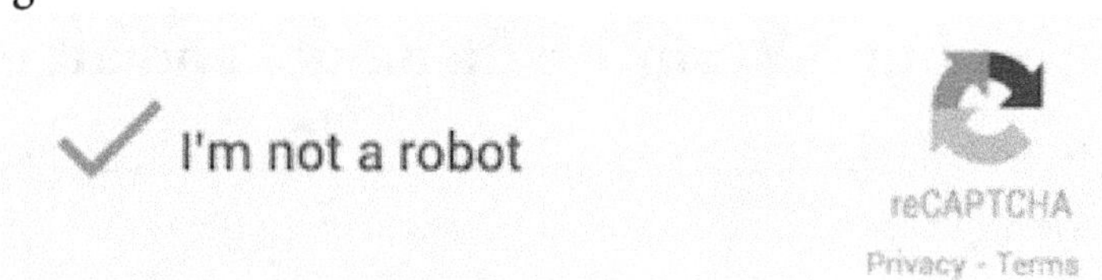

Optimize your images

Use HTML images

Use HTML image elements to embed images in your content.

Use HTML elements <img>**or**<picture>

Semantic HTML markup helps crawlers find and process images. Using the element <picture>, you can also specify multiple options for different screen sizes for responsive images. You can also use the attribute loading="lazy"on images to make the page load faster.

To avoid :

- Use CSS code to display the images you want us to index

Use attributealt

PROVIDE A DESCRIPTIVE filename and attribute description altfor the images. The attribute altallows you to specify alt text for the image if it cannot be displayed for some reason.

Why use this attribute? If someone is viewing your site using assistive technologies like a screen reader, the content of the attribute altgives them information about the image.

Also, if you use an image as a link, the "alt" text of that image will be treated the same as the anchor text of a textual link. However, we don't recommend using too many images as links in your site's navigation when text links can serve the same purpose. Finally, optimizing image filenames and "alt" text helps image search projects, like Google Images, better interpret your images.

Use short but descriptive filenames and alt text

LIKE MOST OTHER AREAS of your page that are targeted for optimization, it's best to use short, but descriptive filenames and alt text.

To avoid :

- Use generic filenames like image1.jpg, pic.gifand 1.jpgwhenever possible (if your site has thousands of images, you might consider automating naming)
- Write very long filenames
- Stack keywords in "alt" text, or copy and paste entire sentences

Provide alt text when using images as links

IF YOU DECIDE TO USE an image as a link, filling in its "alt" text lets Google know more about the page the link corresponds to. Think of yourself as writing anchor text for a text link.

To avoid :

- Writing too long "alt" text that would be considered spam
- Only use links in the form of images for navigation in your site

Help search engines find your images

AN image sitemap provides Google with more information about the images on your site. This makes them more likely to appear in Google Images results. The structure of this file is similar to that of the XML sitemap file of your web pages.

Use standard image formats

USE COMMONLY ACCEPTED file types. Most browsers accept JPEG, GIF, PNG, BMP and WebP image formats. It's also best if your filename extension matches the file type.

Make your site mobile friendly

OUR WORLD HAS BECOME extremely mobile. Most searches on Google are done from a mobile device. It can be difficult to view and use the classic version of a site on a mobile device. Therefore, having a mobile-friendly website is essential for your online presence. Since late 2016, Google has been conducting experiments to primarily use the mobile version of a site's content for search ranking, structured data analysis, and snippet generation.

Understand the differences between the devices

- **Smartphone** : in this document, the terms "mobile" or "mobile device" refer to smartphones, for example devices equipped with Android, or of the iPhone or Windows Phone type. Mobile browsers are similar to desktop browsers in that they can display much of the HTML5 specification, even though their screen size is smaller and their default orientation is almost always vertical.
- **Tablet** : We consider tablets to be separate devices, so when

we talk about mobile devices, we generally exclude tablets. They often have a larger screen than phones. So if you don't offer tablet-optimized content, users will expect to see your site as they would on their computer rather than on their smartphone.

- **Multimedia phone** : These phones are equipped with browsers capable of displaying pages coded according to XHTML standards and accept HTML5 markup as well as JavaScript/ECMAScript scripts. However, they may not be compatible with some extension APIs of the HTML5 standard. This generally concerns the browser of most 3G phones that are not smartphones.
- **Feature phone** : Browsers on these phones cannot display normal HTML-encoded web pages. These are, for example, browsers that only display the languages cHTML (iMode), WML, XHTML-MP, etc.

OUR RECOMMENDATIONS are for smartphones, but we encourage owners of media and feature phone-friendly sites to follow the same advice where appropriate.

Choose a mobile strategy

THERE ARE SEVERAL WAYS to make your website mobile-friendly and Google accepts different methods of implementation:

- Responsive Web Design (*recommended*)
- Dynamic dispaly
- Separate URLs

Once you've created a mobile-friendly site, you can use Google's Mobile Optimization Test to see if your site's pages meet the criteria for earning the "Mobile-Friendly" label in search engine results pages. Google search. You can also check the Search Console mobile usability report to troubleshoot mobile usability issues affecting your site.

If your site has a lot of static content (like blog posts or product landing pages) across multiple pages, consider implementing it using Accelerated Mobile Pages (AMP). It is a variation of HTML code that ensures the speed and usability of the site, and can be further accelerated by various platforms, including Google search.

Configure your mobile sites to optimize their indexing

Whichever configuration you choose for your mobile site, consider the following points:

1. If you use dynamic serving or have a separate mobile site, let Google know when a page is formatted for mobile (or if there's an equivalent page formatted for mobile). This helps Google properly present your content to mobile users in search results.
2. If you're using the Responsive Web Design method, use the tag meta name="viewport"to tell the browser how to adjust the content. If you're using dynamic serving, use the "Vary" HTTP header to signal your changes based on the user-agent. If you are using separate URLs, signal the relationship between these two URLs by adding the tag <link>with the rel="canonical"and elements to the page rel="alternate".
3. Your resources must be searchable. Blocking a page's resources can give Google an incomplete picture of your website. This usually happens when your robots.txt file blocks access to all or some of your page resources. If Google doesn't have access to a page's resources, such as CSS, JavaScript, or image files,

we may not detect that the page was created to display and function on mobile browsers. In other words, we may not detect that the page is mobile-friendly and display it incorrectly for mobile users.

4. Avoid common mistakes that frustrate mobile users, like including large videos that can't be played.
5. Mobile pages that provide a poor user experience may be downgraded or displayed with a warning in mobile search results. This is the case, for example, of full-page interstitials on mobile that harm the user experience.
6. Provide full functionality on all devices. Mobile users expect the same features, like comments and checkout, and the same content on all mobile devices compatible with your website. Besides textual content, make sure all important images and videos are embedded and accessible on mobile devices. For search engines, add all structured data and other metadata, such as titles, descriptions, link elements, and other meta tags, to all versions of your pages.
7. Make sure that the structured data, images, videos, and metadata on your desktop site also appear on the mobile site.

Good practices

- Perform a mobile optimization test to see if your website works well on mobile devices based on Google criteria.
- If you use separate URLs for your mobile pages, test both mobile and desktop URLs to verify that the redirect is recognized and can be crawled.

Promote your website

MOST LINKS TO YOUR site will be added incrementally as people discover your content through search or other means and link to it, but we understand that you want to spread awareness of the work you put into creating it. If you promote your new content effectively, people interested in the topic will discover it more quickly. As with most of the points discussed in this document, taking these recommendations to an extreme could actually damage your site's reputation.

Publishing a blog post on your own site is a great way to let your visitors know that you've added content or services. Other website owners who follow your site or the RSS feed may also refer to it.

It can also be beneficial to promote your business or site offline. For example, if you have a professional site, make sure its URL appears on your business cards, letterheads, posters, etc. You can also send recurring newsletters to your customers by mail informing them of new content on your company's website.

If you run a local business, you can claim your business listing to reach more customers on Google Maps and Google Search.

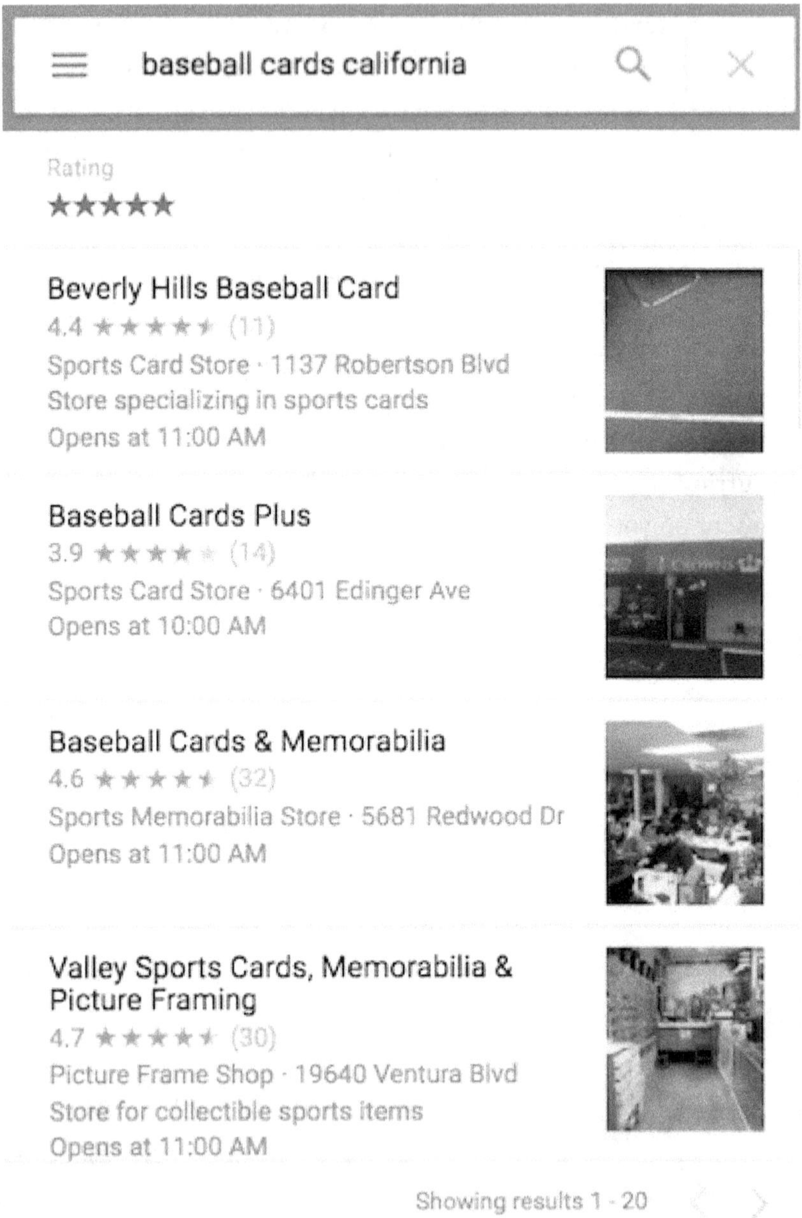
baseball cards california
Rating
Beverly Hills Baseball Card
4.4 (11)
Sports Card Store · 1137 Robertson Blvd
Store specializing in sports cards
Opens at 11:00 AM
Baseball Cards Plus
3.9 (14)
Sports Card Store · 6401 Edinger Ave
Opens at 10:00 AM
Baseball Cards & Memorabilia
4.6 (32)
Sports Memorabilia Store · 5681 Redwood Dr
Opens at 11:00 AM
Valley Sports Cards, Memorabilia & Picture Framing
4.7 (30)
Picture Frame Shop · 19640 Ventura Blvd
Store for collectible sports items
Opens at 11:00 AM
Showing results 1 - 20

Learn about social networking sites

SITES BUILT AROUND user interaction and sharing make it easier to connect groups of people with relevant content.

To avoid :

- Try to promote all the content you create, no matter how insignificant (prefer important and interesting elements)
- Integrate your site into linking systems where your content would be artificially pushed ahead of those services

Connect with members of the community associated with your site

CHANCES ARE THAT THERE are several sites covering similar topics to yours. Connecting with these sites is generally beneficial. Popular topics in your niche or community can provide content ideas or build a resource base for members.

To avoid :

- Abusively send requests to all sites discussing topics related to yours
- Buying links from another site to get a better Page Rank

Analyze search performance and user behavior

Analyze your search performance

THE MAJOR SEARCH ENGINES, including Google, provide tools for website owners to analyze the performance of their sites in search engines. For Google, this is Search Console .

Search Console provides two important categories of information: Is Google able to find my content? How am I performing in Google search results?

Using Search Console does not help your website's results. Instead, it can help you identify issues that, if resolved, can help improve its performance in search results.

With the service, website owners can:

- spot parts of a site that Googlebot has had trouble crawling;
- test and submit sitemaps;
- analyze or generate robots.txt files;
- delete URLs already crawled by Googlebot;
- specify your preferred domain;
- identify issues with Meta tags titleand description ;
- determine the most used searches to access a site;
- get insight into how Google sees pages;
- receive notifications of violations of spam guidelines and request a review of the site.

Among its Bing webmaster tools , Microsoft also offers specific tools for site owners.

Analyze user behavior on your site

IF YOU'VE IMPROVED your site's crawling and indexing using Google Search Console or other services, you probably want to get an idea of your site's traffic. Internet audience analysis programs like Google Analytics are a valuable source of information. You can use them for:

- obtain information relating to the behavior of Internet users on your site and how they access it;

- discover the most popular content on your site;
- measure the impact of optimizations you make to your site (e.g. changing meta tags titleand descriptionhas it improved traffic from search engines?).

If you are an advanced user, you can combine data from your server's log files with an analytics pack to get more comprehensive data on how visitors interact with your documents (e.g. what other keywords they use to find your site).

75 Steps to do SEO and improve your search engine positioning NOW

A Step-by-Step Guide to SEO

Today I am about to share with you 75 keys that you can easily make on your website to increase visitors from search engines. I have tried to order and classify all the steps that I follow myself and the tools that I use the most to do SEO.

I am sure that with this **SEO Manual** you will be able to significantly increase your visits. Because ultimately, good positioning in Google translates into more visits, which is what surely matters to all of us. If you want **to learn more about SEO** , in this article I solve some doubts and answer 50 Questions about SEO .

Learn SEO and web positioning without being an expert programmer

I HAVE TRIED TO SELECT those keys for which a great knowledge of html or editing their own publishing system was not necessary. As the topic of the programming of your page is very important, in most of the ones that I explain are simple changes, or you can help yourself with a Plugin. If you use WordPress , you are in luck.

As it is the most used platform, I have proposed **several Plugins** to position in search engines. In this other article I have compiled some more: "The 40 best WordPress SEO Plugins" . And if after reading this article, with its 75 tips, you feel like learning more and in a more practical way, you can take a look at the new SEO Course that I give in Madrid at Aula CM.

Positioning in Google through Keywords

1. CHOOSE YOUR KEYWORDS well: define for which searches that people do you are going to try to position. Consider the number of searches for each term to find your best keywords. You can use Google Trends to define your natural positioning strategy in Google.

2. Check the competition: You can use the following tool to check not only the number of searches for each keyword, but also the competition they have. So you will know which words are more affordable according to the popularity of your website: Google Adwords Keyword Tool

3. Measure the density of the words: Analyze your page and discover which words you are using the most. Try to repeat more those that you want to position well. Use This Internet Ninja Tool

4. Use keywords: Use them in your texts, labels and categories. The first 200 words of each page have more value, so it is a good idea to make a lead summarizing the article. At the same time as encouraging the rest of the reading, you take the opportunity to position your words.

5. Keywords in titles and bold: If you can, use them to create titles and incidentally to base your content on them. If you can highlight some bold in each article you will make it easier for Google to catalog you.

6. Measure and analyze your natural positioning for different keywords: Check your search engine ranking for all your keywords. You can use the following free tool to install on your computer: CuteRank It will tell you the number of the page you appear on in Google for each search.

Site configuration according to the SEO Manual

7. META DESCRIPTION and title: Define for each page of your website a description and a title in the Meta tags of each heading <head>. These will be the titles and descriptions that are seen on

Google and with which you intend to attract attention. If you use WordPress you can use, for example , All in One SEO Pack . You will have a new SEO editing forms in each article.

8. Friendly and edited URLs: Use a URL writing system that is like your titles. You can shorten and edit them so that they contain the largest number of keywords. In WordPress you can activate this feature in Settings, and you can edit each URL within the edition of each article.

9. Creation and submission of sitemaps to search engines: Sitemaps help search engines to index your site and keep them updated in their cache. Google and Bing have their own pages for you to send your files to. You can use XML Sitemaps Generator

10. Automate the sending of sitemaps: Since we should send sitemaps every time there is a change, it is best to automate it. With WordPress we can do it with the Google XML Sitemaps plugin

11. Transcribe your audiovisual content: The content of your videos or presentations is not indexed by Google so it is a good idea to make a text transcription if you can and find the space.

12. Favicon: The favicon is the small logo that appears in each tab and in favorites and identifies each website. You can create your own and upload it to your template: http://www.favicon.cc/

13. Avoid the use of cookies: unnecessary requests and problems with data privacy.

14. Use rel=”author”: Configure the authorship of your publications and show the author's image in search engines. It will help draw attention to your articles and give them personality on Google.

Images in search engine positioning

15. TITLE AND DESCRIPTION: Include the ALT and TITLE tags in all Images. If not, the search engines will not know what they are and will not be able to index them. If you are very lazy you can use SEO Friendly Images in WordPress to fill them automatically.

16. Specify its size: Always define the size of the image, either in Html with its width and height tags, or in WordPress when publishing it. If not, the browser will resize the page when the image is filled and it won't look good until it loads completely. Google wants our page to see the sizes as they are going to be from the first moment, not to grow.

17. Do not scale images in Html: Decide what is the size of each image in the article and upload it that size. If we make it smaller with html or the blog editor, it will still have to load big.

18. Optimize images for the web: Use a compressor or save for the web in Photoshop. The highest image quality is not required for the web and images take up a large part of download data. We want the page to load as soon as possible. You can use the Smush it tool on the blog , which allows you to automatically improve the compression of your images.

19. Combine images using CSS sprites: If your template or design uses a lot of small images together, it is recommended that you combine them into a single image and define the links using the sprites in CSS.

Take care of the links for a good web positioning

20. DIVERSIFIED ANCHOR text: These are the words that can be clicked on to visit your website. We must try to get links to us in a descriptive way, using keywords and not always the same, but varying them, making them seem like natural recommendations. You can use: Backlink Anchor Text Analysis

21. Check for broken links: Google hates us if we make it visit broken links. We must avoid it and check all our links regularly, every week. With this online tool it is very simple and it will tell us which ones do not work: InternetMarketingNinjas

22. Avoid redirections: Both on our site and when linking to other pages. The previous tool will also tell us which links have to be redirected to another address and suggests that we shorten the steps.

23. Automate the search for broken links: We can use a WordPress plugin to notify us when a link stops working: Broken Link Checker

24. Know the PageRank: It is the evaluation that Google makes from 0 to 10 of each site on its positioning and authority. Know and measure the evolution of your PageRank and that of the sites that link to you or propose link exchange. You can use http://pgchecker.info

25. Do not link malicious or illegal content: Google penalizes pages that link content with viruses or declared pirates.

26. Look where your competition links: Learn from their strategy while you find new ways to get links and improve positioning.

27. Use internal links: Find where to highlight other parts of your website and get used to linking your articles to each other naturally.

We avoid Duplicate Content

28. ORIGINAL TEXTS: Check that all your texts are original. If this is not the case, Google will be the first to know and will rate your page negatively. You can use Copyscape .

29. No-index to our duplicate content: We will add the no-index tag to our pages where our content is repeated: the categories, archive by dates and tags. With All in One SEO Pack we can configure it in WordPress.

30. Initial page with only sample: We will not include the full text of the articles on the initial page of our blog, only a sample part and a Read More link. Otherwise, Google will have duplicates of the same texts and the article itself only it will no longer have exclusive content.

31. Description and Meta Title without repeating: In the descriptions for the search engines we cannot have any repeated ones either because it would create another conflict for the search engines.

32. Canonical URL: Check that your web address is canonical: http://brunovd.com and http://www.brunovd.com

33. The same design for web and mobile It is preferable to use an adaptable or Responsive design that allows us to have the same design for all devices. If we have two different versions, search engines will find duplicate content and they will have to have two parallel copies of the site.

Your Web positioning Style Guide

34. CREATE FUN AND ORIGINAL content: Make these make the reader spend more time on your page and see other pages of the site. Google is increasingly taking into account the factors of usability and permanence on your website, so the biggest trick is to be great and worthy of mention. Study the times and the bounce rate of each article to learn what your readers prefer.

35. Long content: If your page is 4 paragraphs, the reader will not last much more than 20 seconds. Try to make more ambitious content and you will be able to retain the reader for longer. Of course, without going overboard, because you could fall into the opposite error and significantly increase the loading time of the page.

36. Take care of your visitors from devices: Visits from mobile phones and tablets are an important part of the statistics and you have to take care of the usability and presentation of your page for these resolutions. If you want them to spend more time on your page, you must have an adaptable design or, failing that, a mobile web version. You can check your website for all resolutions and devices with this tool: Screenfly

37. Publish regularly: Search engines appreciate that your website is updated and alive. Try to post at least weekly to be listed as an active source of information. If your website is static, try to create a blog section that you can publish more frequently and create Landing Pages to attract different types of search engine searches.

38. Participate and connect with your community: It will be the best way to be linked and mentioned. Help others and answer questions in comments. Interact and participate with the community interested in your content. If you need to review ideas in Social Media, I recommend the Community Manager's Manual in 8 free guides .

39. Protocol after each article: After publishing each article, execute a protocol of actions that you perfect over time. This should take about 20 minutes and it is very important to do it after each article or page is published. We could publish on Twitter, Facebook, Pinterest, G+, Linkedin Groups, forums in which you participate, comments on related articles, directories, favorite aggregators... All the initial work is good to get some first links on websites and shares on social networks . Your articles are always more visible in search engines in the first 4 days, so the initial push helps increase visits on those better days.

40. Guest Blogging: Write an article on other guest blogs. You can make yourself known in other spaces and also get quality links to your website. In many blogs they accept it or you can propose it. For example, if you write about marketing and Social Media you can send your articles to Puromarketing .

41. Offer some valuable content: Prepare and offer some content that you offer from a landing page that they can link to and you can monitor the visits. Try to make it necessary to go to your page to access the content. It is a good idea to combine it with the use of other tools such as Pay with a Tweet or subscription by mail with Mailchimp .

42. Landing Page: Do specific SEO work for the different Landing Pages that you can create to find different ways to attract people to your website. Position content for certain keywords and monitor the visits you receive to that page through search engines.

43. Take care of the reader: Remove, for example, that unnecessary publicity that is not giving you any money from your website. You will save loading time and improve the usability of your page.

Avoid Google Penalties

44. DO NOT PUT KEYWORDS out of context: Do not use a technique of putting keywords massively in text without any sense to increase density or receive visits.

45. Do not put hidden text: Google strongly penalizes the technique of writing text that the reader does not see, under images, videos or other layers, in order to position certain terms.

46. Avoid code errors that you can: Search engines prefer those pages with code that meets the standards and will look correct for most situations. The best way we have to know how correct our code is, is to use the W3C Markup Validator tool.

47. Do not go too far with the exchange of links: It is not bad to have some (between 5 and 20) exchange links with other pages, as long as they are of a topic very similar to ours and there is real participation between the two. I advise against creating large collections of links exchanged with other websites on various topics or different specialties. The best of all will be the ones you win because you deserve them.

Reduce the loading time of your page and Google will love you very much

48. MEASURE AND IMPROVE the speed of your page: It is another of the most important factors for good positioning and we can use several tools to measure it. With Google Page Speed it will tell us many points where we can improve our speed. Another widely used tool is the Yslow Chrome application , which will also give us many recommendations.

49. Do not abuse javascript codes: Check how many javascripts your page uses and try to save on those that are not very necessary. We like to put a lot of functions and effects into websites, without taking into account the weight that this entails.

50. Delete WordPress plugins: Uninstall all the plugins you don't use and try to save the ones you can. Evaluate in each case the functions that it offers you and the size and work that they give to the web each time they are loaded. From 600kb of data in javascript in the load of your main page, it starts to be too much. You can know which plugins weigh more with P3 Plugin Profiler . In the WordPress Course that I give, we install and test many plugins, but then we also have to analyze their speed and remove most of them that are not really useful. In our WordPress Course in Aula CM we install and test many plugins, but in the end it is always time to evaluate which one is worth staying with.

51. Put javascript at the end of the code: Try to place the javascript load as far back in the code as possible. If it has to be at the head, let it be at the end. If it can be in the body, in the end too. This will prevent the page from waiting to display the contents until it has loaded the java.

52. Delay or defer javascript loading: You can use html and java code to force javascript plugins to load at the end. In WordPress we have this component that helps us load our heavier plugins after displaying the page content: Lazy Widget Loader

53. Save and clean your code: Your code is not what occupies the most, but it is opened many times. You can clean your html, css and php files from unnecessary annotations and compress them with the help of some tool.

54. Minify Your Css and Java-Script: You can use the Minify tool for any web page to combine and minify your Css and Java-Script files. In WordPress you can access it through the W3 Total Cache plugin .

55. Combine your Javascripts: If you have more than 3 or 4 javascripts that are loaded on all pages, it is a very good idea to combine them in a single file and you will save requests and time. Perhaps it is the part of the article in which more knowledge is needed, but with a very basic idea of java they will know how to put it together. In WordPress you can use JS & CSS Script Optimizer

56. Use pagination: If your content is very long and for blog article submissions, we must paginate the content so that it is not too long and heavy. The blog page should be limited to 5 or 6 articles, and always just a sample or headline, not full.

57. Reduce the number of DNS queries: Try not to link to or load images from many different domains. Try to make all http requests to your same domain. Otherwise it would take a long time to resolve the different requests and the loading time would greatly increase

58. Few http calls: It is recommended that our pages make the fewest possible number of requests to the server. I recommend that you do not exceed 25. The GtMetrix tool will measure and analyze this data.

59. Compress in gzip: We must enable compression in gZip, which is like the Zip of the web code. Browsers download and process it faster so today it is essential to use it. In WordPress we can enable it with the previously mentioned W3 Total Cache plugin .

60. Use page cache: The cache is like a copy of the page that the reader saves so they don't have to load it the next time they ask for it. There are several types of cache systems. With W3 Total Cache or other plugins they can help you, with images too. Page speed will increase noticeably in all cases.

61. Use cache for Java-Script: We have agreed that the java-script plugins are the heaviest part of the web with images, so if we cache them we will also save many times their load.

62. Determine a cache expiration date: We can manually configure the validity of the cache, depending on the type of file. We will set the variables with mod_expires and .htaccess . If we don't, you may ask for the data too often or almost never. For images and javascript we can give you an expiration date of 3 weeks and for text 3 days. In WordPress, W3 Total Cache will help us .

63. Use a CDN: A content delivery network is a system by which visitors enter a parallel copy of your website hosted on another server. We benefit from protection, speed, cached copies and more features.

You will need to be able to make some server changes to your DNS names. We can use, for example, the free version of CloudFlare

64. Do not use nested tables in html: It is quite common to fall into the error of using one table within another, but it can slow down our page a lot. Sometimes it is not easy to realize and we can discover it with W3C Markup Validator

65. External css and not styles in the code. It is very common to apply the styles directly on the page and not in an external CSS file. If you use WordPress it will also happen to you. Try to use the predefined styles that you have on the right of the editor, and if not try to write in the HTML tab and apply the styles that you have defined in your Css. You will save loading time and efficiency to make changes.

66. External Java script and not inside the code. We also used to see a lot of html and php code with javascript inside. It will always be preferable to link it from an external file, which in turn we can combine with others, save in cache and minimize if possible.

67. Check the loading times of each page: Analyze loading times and their bounce, and test and measure different alternatives to improve usability. You can use GtMetrix again .

Essential tools to start with good SEO

68. Woorank: A very complete tool to initially analyze our website. WooRank.com

69. Web Ceo: An online paid tool, but with a fairly complete free version. It will help us to monitor our links and keywords, at the same time that we can contrast the data with Google Analytics. Web CEO Online

70. Screaming Frog: A tool to install on the computer. It analyzes and tracks our website as if it were a search engine and allows us to improve failures. Screaming Frog SEO Spider Tool & Crawler Software

71. All in One SEO Pack: The most complete plugin for your SEO WordPress. It will allow us to do a multitude of functions that we have discussed in this article. All in One SEO Pack

72. SEO by Yoast: Another alternative to the previous one, with many possibilities and functions to improve our search engine positioning. WordPress SEO by Yoast

73. W3 Total Cache: It is the most used Cache plugin in WordPress and it is wonderful. There are other alternatives, but this is very very complete. It will help us improve the speed of our website. W3 Full Cache

74. SEO Chat Seo Tools: It is the largest collection of free tools online to do SEO. Surely by testing your website you will get some useful information.

And the last step for a good SEO search engine positioning

75. Leave me a comment and link your blog: Participation with the community is the most important point of all. If we want to get recommendations we will have to connect with the people who make them. If your contribution is interesting you will get visits from other readers. I will probably visit your blog and maybe I will link to you or share you on social networks. And in any case, at least Google will have linked our blogs and noted our relationship and participation.

SEO guide for ecommerce Improve your organic positioning!

Working on SEO in your e-commerce on a recurring basis is one of the almost mandatory tasks today if you want to be competitive on the Internet.

In order to (at least) aim to be among the first search results, you must use all the artillery at your disposal.

And far from what you are thinking...

You can improve the organic positioning of an online store by applying very simple techniques!

Of course, you need 2 basic ingredients:

- Follow the advice in this guide from start to finish.
- And big doses of patience, since SEO is a long-term career. If

you are patient you will see the results.

Do you have these two ingredients?

SO COME WITH ME AND discover what to work to make Google fall in love with your online store and you **can stand out from your competition** .

We start:

REVEALING FIGURES ON why optimize SEO in your online store

Let's be honest: if you have entered here looking for how to improve the positioning of your business, it is because your sales have not yet taken off.

Furthermore, we both know that having the best product in the world is a guarantee, but if no one sees or visits you, sales will not come on their own.

And then **your ecommerce runs the risk of having its days numbered!**

To begin with, you may already know that SEO, or "Search Engine Optimization", are all those **techniques aimed at improving the organic positioning of a business** on the Internet.

Being more specific, with the purpose of (at least) getting positioned on the first page of Google , where almost 90% of the users who use this search engine find what they are looking for.

Therefore, before you learn about the SEO techniques that you can apply in your store, you should reflect on these enlightening facts:

⟐ Google continues to be the most used search engine in the world, with a market share of 92% . They are followed by Bing and Yahoo with a dismal 2-3%

⟐ Around 80% of users only **pay attention to the first page** of results.

⟐ As of today, almost 90,000 Google searches are performed **every second! Someone is looking for you and hasn't found you yet.**

◈ In Spain, 95% of citizens use this search engine on their mobile devices and 99% use it as a first alternative.

You will therefore understand that in this article, when we talk about search engines, we are referring to Google, right?

SEO factors to improve the organic positioning of your ecommerce

1. Keyword Research or search for your main keywords
2. Choose the “Long tail” keywords to grow
3. Be specific with what you want to sell
4. Create a solid (and logical) web architecture
5. Optimize your product listing
6. Take care of the photographs of your products
7. Avoid discontinued product pages
8. SEO On Page basic to take into account
9. Make social networks your best ally
10. Get a good external link
11. Boost your "local SEO" if you also have a physical store

Before starting, you should keep in mind that there is a lot of competition on the Internet in most sectors, **in yours too!**

Image by Diggity Marketing from Pixabay

And even if you think that your competitors are only the entrepreneurs of the ecommerce sector who are looking to gain a foothold in Google, like you, several “major players” also come into play, such as:

→ **Amazon, Aliexpress, eBay** , or some local or regional brand quite "settled" in your business niche.

However, I am sure that in passion and desire you beat all of them. Still if you want to test your knowledge of positioning before starting:

Let's go step by step.

1. Keyword Research or search for your main keywords

ALTHOUGH THERE ARE hundreds of factors that the search engine takes as criteria to classify the contents , one of the priorities is the keywords.

And, how do I search for my keywords or the way in which my potential customers search on Google?

IN SEO TERMS THIS IS what is called doing a Keyword Research. A study through which you can reach different conclusions to improve the SEO of your ecommerce.

PASO 1

MAKE A LIST OF THE words or terms for which you would like to appear in Google and their variants.

PASO 2

THE NEXT STEP IS TO ensure that those terms have real searches in the search engine. I eat? using tools that give you this data.

You have paid or free.

PASO 3

MAKE A LIST IN EXCEL with all the words of your study and assign them to the pages of your store.

REMEMBER

FOR EACH URL OF YOUR store, work on a main keyword (whether it is a product file, a category, a blog article,...). Otherwise, you will fall into keyword cannibalization.

That is, if you have a category that you want to position for "non-stick pans" do not use this word again to write a blog post.

Otherwise you will have two pages competing within your same store.

PASO 4

SEPARATE THE COMMERCIAL keywords from the informative ones : you must work with the commercial ones with your products; the others can be the perfect "excuse" to have a powerful blog.

For example:

- Commercial keyword: “buy crossfit shoes”
- Informative keyword: "why special shoes are necessary in crossfit"

2. Choose the “Long tail” keywords to grow

A COMMON MISTAKE THAT entrepreneurs like you often make is getting carried away by “vanity metrics”.

They begin to target keywords that are too generic and with very high search volumes with their content.

But you have an advantage!

BECAUSE YOU ARE READING this article and you are going to discover what happens with high search volume words.

Try searching Google for a very generic term related to online sales. See what happens:

Let's say you are a shoe store.

→ DO YOU THINK YOU will be able to fight to be in the TOP1 with companies like “El Corte Inglés”, Zalando, Marypaz or Catchalot...?

In a few years, hopefully so, but right now it would be "the chronicle of a death foretold."

You have to take another path: that of the long tail , those terms made up of 4 or more words.

Do you need an example?

Continuing with our theme:

◈ **“women's shoes”** : has about 12.1k monthly searches and generates 227 Million results on Google

◈ **"comfortable shoes to work long hours on your feet for women"** : it only has about 320 searches and activates 912k results

From this comparison it can be deduced that the second term, having much less content in the Google ranking pointing to that query, search, will (in theory) have less competition.

Therefore it is easier for you to **find a gap between so many giants** in your sector.

The key to the use of long tails in SEO for ecommerce is in the following point. Keep reading...

3. Be specific with what you want to sell

HOW CONCISE AND SPECIFIC you are in the content that you include in each of your pages will lead the search engine to understand its context better or worse.

Make it clear which product you want to focus on within each URL and Google will be clear for which keyword to rank your content.

Thus, you can offer the user your page as high as possible.

Otherwise, if you mix 2 products or concepts on the same page, it will not position you for one or the other...

You have seen that " **for each URL, there is only one main keyword to work** with ", right?

Now that you know something more about the use of keywords and, since we are going to specify even more, I will also be more specific:

For each URL on your website, use one (and only one) search intent

THE CONCEPT OF SEARCH intent has to do with knowing with what specific intention the user is searching for a keyword or phrase.

You may be typing a keyword in the search engine with the intention of buying, finding out information, solving a very specific question, etc.

Go ahead and create content that satisfies that search!

WE CAN BE AS SPECIFIC in our way of explaining things as the varieties of the product in question we have in our e-commerce.

" Increase in voice searches

More than 20% of users already use voice searches, which are carried out in a more specific way"

So be as specific as possible.

With the language so rich and varied, you can play with **variations of Spanish** in a thousand and one ways.

Do you want an example?

THE "INTELLIGENCE" of Google today allows it to know that you are talking about something without having to repeat that term so many times.

Without going any further, if you write about "SEO", you can enrich your content by going to synonyms and concepts that mean the same thing:

- "Organic positioning"
- "Natural positioning in search engines"
- “Search Engine Optimization”
- "The techniques to position organically"

4. Create a solid (and logical) web architecture

YOUR STORE MUST HAVE a well-ordered hierarchical structure in a logical way.

This order must be applied through your internal link, which will benefit:

- El SEO On-Page in you ecommerce
- And to the experience of the user who visits you

IMAGINE THAT YOUR VISITORS enter your website (either through SEO or SEM) and, after browsing for a few minutes, they don't know where they are or how to get to the product they want.

The normal thing is that they leave your store and go in search of another. **It is as if you enter a supermarket and there is no order in the placement of products. The yogurts are with the fruit, the meat with the fish etc.**

As for Google, a good organization of taxonomies helps their bots to understand much better what, how and why your content is organized that way.

We can see it this way:

1. Home or start page

HERE YOU MUST SHOW the segmentation of the site into categories and highlight the most outstanding products that you have.

2. The categories

THEY DEFINE HOW THE web is divided.

In a clothing store for animals, a small example of the theme ***"T-shirts for cats"*** can be: ***"Blog"***, ***"Brands"***, ***"Breeds"***, ***"Size"***.

3. The subcategories

THEY ARE THOSE THAT complement the categories, for example:

- ***"Razas"*** > Siamese, Sphynx, Angora, Persian, Bengal
- ***"Size"*** > small cat, medium cat, large cat

4. Tags:

LABELS ARE NOT WIDELY used in most cases, but in an ecommerce they can be useful depending on the case.

They serve to establish a common characteristic of various products:

"Red T-shirts" > here you can place all the models of your store regardless of their category:

- ***"Raza"***
- ***"Size"***
- ***"Brand"***

TIP

IF YOU WANT TO FURTHER optimize categories or tags, you can **add text related to the main keyword** of that section. You will make Google take more into account your categories, while avoiding falling into "**Thin Content**" . Pages with little content that do not add value to your online store or Google.

5. Optimize your product listing

WE CONTINUE WITH ANOTHER SEO factor for ecommerce: product pages.

It will be the "**showcase**" **of everything you sell** to your potential customers (and to Google, always keep this in mind...)

Here you will add several photos of the model, its respective title, the price and payment methods, the sharing buttons,...

But what else...?

You must strategically work the description of all your products .

It is time to apply SEO-Copywriting techniques , which will help you:

- Persuade the user that they are reading said description
- Offer original and creative content to Google

This combination is betting on the "winning horse"!

AS FOR THE KEYWORDS you use, remember that they should point to a **commercial intention** , to leave the informative ones for the corporate Blog.

If you are thinking about setting up your own online store

» **Practical tips for your product sheets**

AVOID COPYING THE DESCRIPTION of the manufacturer / supplier:

If the products you sell are previously purchased from the original manufacturer, **forget about "copy/paste"!**

It is a very common mistake that most e-commerce companies fall into, due to laziness or ignorance. Copying the description to your store is duplicate content , **and it's something Google hates!**

Do you want to stand out from your competition?

MAKE EXPLANATORY VIDEOS in which you explain the operation and benefits of your products.

Your customers will love to see them in action! This, in turn, will make them spend more time on your website and your bounce rate will decrease .

⟐ Allow (and encourage) feedback from those who have already bought from you.

It is said in Spain that "when many cars are parked in front of a restaurant, the food is good".

Well, the same thing happens in your e-commerce: positive comments will be the best magnet for those who are still thinking about it.

6. Take care of the photographs of your products

THE IMAGES YOU USE in your online store are also "main players" in the SEO of an ecommerce.

More and more people are searching for images on Google, so appearing in the first results will give you extra organic visibility.

Sample of the details that Google's Open images V6 is capable of capturing

Did you know...?

GOOGLE HAS BEEN EXPERIMENTING with AI applied to images for years, in its project: Open Images V6 . This is capable of describing in detail what is seen in a photo.

This makes it clear that the quality of your photos must be the best possible.

Thus, the algorithm will capture all the details and will be able to have an exact description of them.

And if you also apply a correct optimization of the images on your part, it will also position them in the first results for related queries.

» Whenever you upload images to your website, check this checklist:

1. File name:

MAKE SURE IT'S AS DESCRIPTIVE as possible, but not too long.

Separate each term with a hyphen (-) and try to contain the main keyword or derivatives.

For example: “red-heeled-shoes.jpg”

Avoid those of the type "IMG001.jpg" that the cameras offer you by default! It is a very common SEO error (but it continues to be repeated every day in online stores)

2. The ALT attribute:

IN THIS HTML TAG YOU must include a short description of what is seen in the image, if possible also including some interesting keyword.

It will be the text that your users will see when they hover over them and it will also influence whether they can appear in Google image searches .

3. Size

IF POSSIBLE, YOU SHOULD upload images to your website exactly in the size in which the end user views them. Neither bigger nor smaller.

Otherwise, the browser will have to scale them to adapt them to the final size visible on the screen.

Something that will slow down the loading time of the URLs that contain them, negatively impacting the WPO of the web.

4. Weight

ANOTHER DECISIVE FACTOR that, if excessive, will also make your website load slower.

Here we recommend that none exceed 100kb.

To lighten the weight of your photos there are many tools. My favorite is TinyPNG , give it a try!

7. Avoid discontinued product pages

DO YOU HAVE PRODUCTS removed from your store that you are never going to sell again?

→ These URL's **will continue to be indexed in the search engine** for a while (check it in Google Search Console).

The best thing you can do is 301 redirect them to another item. It will be a good suggestion towards another product with equivalent characteristics.

You can also **apply the 301 to the main** product category, where you can freely choose a different one.

Otherwise, they will generate a 404 error for page not found, something that will harm the SEO of your ecommerce in the long run.

Many online stores choose to implement a creative custom 404 error page, along with an internal search engine .

This allows your visitors to search for another similar product within your catalog

Custom 404 page on HawkersCo, with link to "best sellers" and home

8. Basic SEO On Page to take into account

WITHIN YOUR WEBSITE you can make some adjustments that, however small they may be, can boost the SEO of your e-commerce in a big way in the medium term:

» Metatitle:

The SEO title will be the one that search engines will see when you appear in the search results, also in SEM results

If you manage to create creative and original titles , you will be able to increase the CTR of your pages and blog articles, which will benefit your positioning:

A whole chain reaction to improve your organic visibility!

» METADESCRIPTION

It is an element that is not a direct indicator that favors SEO, but an indirect indicator: **it improves the CTR** , which it is.

It makes your search result more "palatable" to click, so writing attractive meta descriptions will earn you points.

9. Make social networks your best ally

HAVING AN ACTIVE PRESENCE on social networks helps you boost the SEO of your online store.

Yes, **just as you read it!**

The web traffic that comes from social networks is qualified as " Social SEO ", highly valued by search engines.

Think that most platforms are overcrowded, that appearing in the internal searches of each network is complicated.

In addition, for a few years, Google has also positioned in its SERPs some results from social networks that it considers relevant.

Try to carry out any search of the type "how to do...". **You almost certainly come across a YouTube video!**

That is to mention the good treatment that the search engine gives to the contents of Pinterest with everything related to products and trending themes , such as decoration, recipes, fashion, etc.

10. Get a good external link

OFF PAGE SEO CAN BE summarized as all the efforts you make externally to position your website.

It is an essential factor in SEO for ecommerce, but why?

Because Google considers that a website is relevant if many people are talking about it. And how does Google measure this? through links received from external websites.

Of course, not everything is fine. In other words, the important thing is that whoever talks about us is related to the subject.

See here how to do effective link building

IN FACT, GOOGLE HAS an algorithm " **Google Penguin** ", which pursues ways to get unethical links , artificially created with the aim of climbing positions in the rankings "at all costs".

Also, very suspiciously, these links are in most cases built with an exact anchor text , in order to rank for the keyword of interest...

You can even receive negative SEO attacks that could ruin all your efforts.

Do you want to know better ways to get links and thus improve the SEO of your ecommerce?

To avoid "fraudulent techniques" or "unethical" links, take note of how to get "recommendations" in a better way.

Guest Blogging Posting

ARTICLES ON SPECIALIZED blogs in your sector and with great authority is one of the most recurring strategies.

In addition to allowing you to make contacts within your professional area, **most of them will allow you to include a link** to your online business blog.

And if over time you accumulate a large number of backlinks from your same topic, it will have a favorable impact on an increase in your domain authority .

Linkbaiting

WE COULD TALK LONG and hard about it, since it is considered one of the best "White Hat" techniques of SEO Off-Page.

Summing up quite a bit, it consists of **your content being so, so good** , that users want to link to it voluntarily.

It's that simple? Without us doing anything? As it is.

WE USUALLY REFER TO it when talking about blog articles , due to their informative content.

However, it could also be applicable to your product pages, as long as they are original and creative, why not?

Thus, almost without wanting to, SEO will be helping you to get more clients .

◈ Network and get out of your website into the real world!

WHEN WE TALK ABOUT SEO for ecommerce, if I recommend that you do online public relations and practice " Outreach ", you will think I am crazy, right?

Not at all! Creating strategic and, why not, friendly ties within your same sector only has advantages... also for SEO.

It will help you to listen to the opinions of other professionals who have their businesses on other ecommerce platforms , it will make you broaden your sights.

And also, through these contacts, you will make them know about your business and visit you, with the possibility that, when the time comes, they prefer to link to you instead of another, and thus, by the way, strengthen that new "bond".

Position your ecommerce and increase your conversions thanks to Álex Serrano, put on your headphones and hit Play!

11. Boost your "local SEO" if you also have a physical store

IT MAY BE THAT IN ADDITION to your own online store, you have a store at street level where you offer your products.

In that case, creating a Google My Business listing is your next step! It may also be called " Google My Business " in your country *(you can find it by any of these meanings).*

It will allow you to appear geolocated in the search results of people who want to buy products like the ones you offer, while being physically in the immediate vicinity of your location.

To position yourself in local results, here are some tips:

- Encourage positive reviews in your local
- Use Local Search tools
- Always have your ecommerce adapted to mobile devices , since a large part of these searches are carried out at street level
- Find your business and analyze your local SEO yourself. "Put yourself in the shoes" of your potential client and make the changes that you think are pertinent

THESE WILL BE POSITIVE signs to improve your local SEO strategy and, in turn, improve the SEO of your ecommerce in general.

It is time to get down to work with the SEO of your online store

AS YOU HAVE SEEN, IMPROVING the SEO of your ecommerce depends on many factors. Forget that only with the name you put your online store you will get to appear in Google.

Getting to appear in the first 10 pages of the search engine or appear in the TOP3 takes many hours of work in the "backstage".

But, I have good news for you!

THIS SEO GUIDE FOR your online store is the first step to become part of the first results in the search engine.

After all, they are tips that you can implement yourself without the need for an SEO analyst or specialist in the field.

All of them will also help you to position a PDF or any other type of downloadable that you offer and indicate it as indexable within the web.

You only need basic knowledge of the online world and keep up to date with the latest updates of the Google algorithm .

SEO for social networks: good practices to position your business

Here we will talk about SEO for social networks, but we cannot start without first remembering what SEO is. These acronyms stand for Search Engine Optimization, which translates to search engine optimization.

What intention do you have? Well, position a website in the first places of Google (or some other search engine) and, from there, generate endless benefits that meet the objectives of a brand or client.

For a few years something very particular has been sounding: **"SEO for social networks"**; This has immediately raised several questions, including: Is SEO important for social media, or does it directly influence organic results?

The answer, although it is not so simple, makes it very clear what you want to aim for with these new practices: to do it so well in each digital space that your brand does not leave gaps in the quality of everything it offers to users.

What is SEO for social networks or social SEO?

SEO FOR SOCIAL NETWORKS is the union of SEO and Social Media strategies, with the intention of generating new practices to improve the visibility of a brand.

The term "social" is given to it, because it is not the SEO that properly positions a website in those search engine results, but because "it goes from social networks to a website".

Its main objective is to positively impact users, through well-optimized content, which seeks to take the target audience from the networks, to a specific URL of the target page or website.

Basically, they behave as a very essential part of any digital Marketing strategy .

What elements indicate a positive evolution in the SEO strategy for social networks?

IN THIS CASE WE WILL talk about **social signals,** indicators that refer to user interactions, emotions and relationships with the content they consume on the networks.

You may ask yourself: "what are those telltale signs within a social media ecosystem?" Here we list them:

- Followers and their quality. The more followers are interested in your brand, the better it will be.
- Interactions (comments, shares, likes, pins, mentions, etc.)
- Engagement (the commitment of users to a brand)
- Age of the profiles (in this sense, profiles of old data will have accumulated a greater number of visits and interactions. It happens, in the same way, as with a website, since it influences positively, as long as it involves good practices)
- Backlinks: those direct links to a website or a blog with which we seek to meet business objectives: traffic, conversions, recognition, sales, etc.

Do social signals influence the positioning of a web page?

NOT DIRECTLY. THESE signals certainly do not influence an SEO strategy to position a website in Google . However, by making correct use of social platforms, we will be able to involve the public that interests us and promote our brand. This is where a considerable impact is made on certain factors that drive rankings on Google.

Mainly by delivering quality content to the user on a regular basis (we'll talk about this later), we will achieve an increase in participation/interaction of those future customers with our brand content, progressively generating greater awareness about it.

The intention is to make the best use of social networks, to positively influence the conversion rates we need for our website.

Do social networks position websites in search results?

We must make this question clear, and it is the definitive "no", which leads as an answer.

AS WE SAID BEFORE, social networks alone will not position your website in Google. That will not happen. At least currently there is no absolute and direct relationship from one point to another. What will happen is that, from the good image that a user takes from the heart of your brand's social networks, a positive (if you do it well) or negative (if you don't) perception will be generated, which will influence on what you want to achieve with your website: conversion, traffic, sales, etc.

For Google, social networks are "independent", and they would have nothing to do with what impacts the positioning of their results, in principle, but it has become clear that the more virality of content and the more interest in it by users , greater brand awareness we will be generating, which does directly benefit your business.

The particularity of Facebook and Twitter in Google results

IT MUST BE BORNE IN mind that Google particularly considers virality on Facebook and Twitter as something that can define content as "interesting or relevant" so that it appears in search results.

According to Matt Cutt, who was the director of the department against Google's web SPAM (and therefore, is part of those who decide if a web page should be higher up or if it is a page that does not contribute anything other than SPAM) , made it known that Facebook and Twitter are considered as two more websites within the

Internet. If something happens in them that makes many users talk about it, Google could crawl it and consider it relevant and thus, it would show it in its results.

How does social media impact SEO?

THIS IS WHERE THE GOOD stuff begins, and if you got here it is because you are looking to improve your content and we love that!

All the links that you share through your social networks and quality content will significantly increase the exposure of your brand on the platforms, and with this you will obtain positive results that will be reflected in the search engines.

Virality and engagement: what attracts Google's attention

WHEN MANY (TOO MANY) people share content, that content could be defined as "viral" and it is precisely this that causes social signals to appear indicating that content is important to a large number of users; This is where Google turns on its radar and says: "This content is possibly very useful."

In turn, these actions have an impact on another social signal that would be engagement, which we know as an indicator with which we can know that level of commitment and interaction of users with the content we publish.

To achieve an impact on both indicators, everything boils down to something fundamental: creating a content marketing strategy for social networks.

How can SEO for social networks help a brand?

By adapting your social media strategy with an SEO approach, you can benefit in different ways:

- It will increase the visibility of your digital channel or social platform (your online visibility)
- It will improve the relevance indicators of your brand.
- It will boost the reach of the content.
- It will increase traffic to your website.

- It will generate engagement from your audience
- It will maintain traffic to the content that interests you the most on your website.
- It will increase the possibility of disseminating more quality content.
- It will improve the online reputation of your brand.

SEO for social networks: creating the strategy

NOW THE BEST PART BEGINS where we will tell you (and show you) what should be done to have a strategy focused on SEO for social networks.

We agree that the basis of any strategy is to align content with business objectives, right? If you answered "no", there is a problem there. That is the first thing we must keep in mind.

Every brand or business has objectives:

- Increase sales
- Improve traffic to your website
- Increase your conversions
- Create brand recognition or brand awareness
- Be a reference in your sector, among others.

EACH STEP WE TAKE WHEN CREATING content for networks must be focused on reaching each of the objectives.

yes, as a first step, you should set your positioning goals for social networks.

So, let's start with this:

1 – Choose well the social networks in which you want to position your brand:

NOT ALL BRANDS NEED to be present on all social networks, nor are all social networks for all brands. Analyzing which network would benefit your business takes a bit of work. Here we could review what the competition is doing, see what is working, take it as a reference, see what they are missing, and start.

The main social networks that are handled the most are:

Facebook

LET'S MAKE IT CLEAR here once and for all. Facebook is the social network that wears the crown, with which it all begins. Why? Because this network also integrates Instagram, Facebook Ads campaigns are activated from it and therefore company pages must be constantly updated.

Twitter

THE SOCIAL NETWORK of immediacy. The last minute information spreads through Twitter in an excessive way; It is the news platform since the beginning of time, the one with controversial conversations and attractive threads that hook anyone. Keeping your profile updated, and sharing quality content with links is basically what is necessary to do SEO on this platform.

instagram

IT BEGAN AS THE SOCIAL network "for photos" and today there is the possibility of selling from Instagram Shopping. The application of SEO strategies for social networks on this platform is limited; it focuses more on creating relevant content with brilliant copy and captions and not so much on generating backlinks. The options that we have on Instagram to share a link are: looking at the bio of the profile or from the link in the stories.

The use of these options within the platform helps to increase traffic, conversions or sales on any web page.

Linkedin

IT IS CURRENTLY THE social network that can bring the most traffic to a website. It is the business network par excellence, with real users and where quality content predominates over other social networks. Here, sharing links is super simple, which is why it is one of the networks that currently benefits the positioning of a company the most.

Youtube

THE SOCIAL NETWORK of videos. Where you can capture your target audience faster if you make good content or you can scare them away in less than 5 seconds if you don't capture their attention and lose points.

Applying SEO to this social network is relatively simple, but it also takes super work behind it, like everything that generates good results: keyword search, striking and not very long titles in the videos, inserting tags (labels) in the audiovisuals, writing attractive descriptions, interlinking between videos with an eye-catching anchor text, optimized profile, etc.

pinterest

IT IS SAID TO BE THE best social network for SEO. In this network, traffic to a web page can be activated through images. Having an account on this network with relevant content (preferably evergreen) increases the chances of appearing in search results, in this case with images.

To apply SEO in this network, it is considered: choosing the appropriate pins for the brand, placing links in the profile, creating boards to save the images (these can also be positioned with keywords in their names), interaction with followers, linking images from a brand website to your Pinterest account.

2 – Analyze how the environment of each social network behaves :

CHECK CAREFULLY WHAT type of content is shared on each social network. What works for one probably won't work for others. Or perhaps some content could work across all just by changing the way it is presented: infographics, video, carousels, text only, etc.

See how they share the content: the frequency, the hours, whether or not they take advantage of any trend at the moment; It also takes into account what the public values on social networks, what content they like the most.

Consider how much your competition does: events, raffles, courses, if it offers downloadable supplies, surveys, among others.

3 – Manage a keyword with which you want to position:

AS AT THE BEGINNING of any SEO strategy or audit to position a website , the search for keywords that respond to the needs and business objectives is an essential step for any strategy to work.

Social networks also need your keywords. Find them, choose them and share them.

4 – Create and share quality content

WHEN PREPARING CONTENT for networks, the process should be exactly the same as if you were writing a super article: you must research, organize your ideas and create good material.

It is extremely important to make it easier for the user to love the publications, so you should never forget that interesting, visually attractive content must be created, taking into account the importance of creating a charming copy, a good design in the graphic pieces and a correct structure. of the texts (captions) that accompany these pieces.

Here you must also be very clear about what type of content you are going to share, such as:

- Articles from your blog.
- ebooks
- Videos
- Static pieces – carousels
- infographics
- podcast

The magic of links from social networks:

THE LINKS MUST BE A key piece within the content that is published on the social networks of a brand, why? because with them we seek to take users to the URL that we are interested in showing within a web page, in addition to helping us to index URLs faster on many occasions .

If you want them to know about your services, you take the user to the home page of your website, or to that internal page that deals with a specific service; if you want to generate conversion, you will take it to the url where it will do the action you are looking for; If your content is purely informative or educational, you will bring traffic to the article within your blog and so on. You can never forget to include a link in your posts.

5 – Optimize your profiles on social platforms

NEGLECTING THE DESCRIPTIONS in the profiles of our networks (the biography on Twitter, for example) can cost us dearly. This is one of the easiest steps when applying SEO for social media.

Use your keywords in the username and description of each social network.

Take advantage of the spaces that each network gives you (to a different extent, depending on what corresponds) to describe in the best possible way what your brand does.

Tag the photos you share.

6 – Optimize the content of each publication (before publishing, preferably but also even after, why not?)

TO OPTIMIZE THE CONTENT of each publication, you can make use of the famous **hashtags,** describe the images with **keywords** and in the captions or descriptions use **emojis** , as they are very well received by the public that consumes social networks. Of course, you must know how to choose the best for each social platform.

There is something left to say: let's not forget Social Ads as part of SEO on social networks

POSITIONING IN SOCIAL networks is something that requires effort and continuous review and, above all, it takes time.

Time is key when taking a social network to the top: time to create, time to schedule, time to manage and, above all, to interact.

The results when we seek positioning on social platforms will not be immediate and we must be very clear about it.

At the beginning everything will be a bit slow, but with continued effort you will see great results. Also, to boost our social media strategy, we can invest in Social Ads to boost and highlight our content.

We can define interaction or reach campaigns to meet the objectives with our brand and in this way we would be speeding up the whole process just a little. Of course, to use Ads on social networks, all the steps mentioned above must be followed exactly.

We should never take for granted that just by positioning ourselves through means of payment we are already achieving everything. That is and will be just one option that will give our brand that little boost, within the great strategy with which we seek organic positioning on social networks.

Frequent questions

1 – How does SEO benefit social networks?

SOCIAL SEO MAINLY GENERATES traffic to a website, improves the performance of page or blog content, is an excellent way to generate backlinks, positions profiles on different social networks, and increases trust in brands. Build brand recognition.

2 – How can you do SEO for social networks?

IN PRINCIPLE, FOR EACH social network there are certain techniques to apply within the SEO strategies that influence each of the platforms.

We can group several fundamental points: keep profiles (biographies) updated, have a list of strategic keywords for the business and use them within the content, create quality content (or evergreen) and take advantage of every opportunity to generate backlinks to the website of the brand.

3 – Does SEO for social networks influence the organic positioning of a web page in Google?

IT DOES NOT DIRECTLY influence search engine positioning, but it does indirectly. By positioning your brand on social networks with a good SEO strategy for social media, you will be generating an advantage for your brand with your target audience.

Each content, image, input, update that you deliver, that is of quality, will create brand awareness, generate engagement, increase traffic to your website and thus, efforts will be constantly joined between the virality that we seek in social media, the interest of the users in our content and the SEO work that we do at the same time so that a website appears in the first positions of Google.

10 practical SEO actions to position companies

What is SEO positioning?

Search engine optimization, also known as "SEO" (Search Engine Optimization), is the process that seeks to improve the ranking of a company in Google, Bing, Yahoo, etc.

In other words, the goal of SEO is to get your business website to appear on the **first page** of search results.

SEO positioning is a continuous process and with a little effort on your part, you will be able to configure the **SEO On Page** of your page well and begin to correctly position your company in search engines.

As we will see, **the possibilities in search engine optimization are numerous** and some or others will be applied depending on what your website needs. It will not be the same to carry out an optimization process in a personal blog than in an online store, since the objectives of the visitor will be different in each case.

What is On Page SEO exactly?

SEO ON PAGE IS THE discipline that is responsible for dealing with all the **factors that directly influence the web positioning of a site** . Unlike Off Page SEO, which takes care of everything that is outside of our website and that we cannot control directly (such as the links that reach our site), On Page SEO is what is under our control.

Factors such as the content, the structure of the site, the URL, the title of the pages, among others, are key elements that must be analyzed.

On-page SEO audit

What does a well positioned company do?

TO BE WELL POSITIONED, a company needs a **good SEO strategy** , a good product and a good brand. This means you need to set **clear internet goals** , have a plan and the means to achieve them, and take the actions necessary to meet them. You also need a product or service that is of high quality and meets customer expectations.

Lastly, you need to build a strong and positive brand that builds trust and allows you to stand out from the competition.

Success story SEO client of Te Veo Online

Practical SEO actions to position a company

THERE ARE A NUMBER of techniques and processes to improve the positioning of a web page in search engines. These techniques must be applied correctly and constantly to obtain the best results.

Do you want to learn how to improve the positioning of your company on the internet? Here are 10 actions that will help you:

Keyword research for keyword strategy

KEYWORDS ARE TERMS or phrases that users enter into search engines when searching for something on the internet. And if you want your website to appear in search results for those keywords, **you need to strategically incorporate them into your content** .

You must include these words **naturally and using variants** . Keyword variation is an SEO technique that involves using different forms of the same keyword to improve rankings in search results.

In the following screenshot you can see an example of a keyword analysis to identify the best keywords:

Keyword Research Example

HERE ARE SOME TOOLS for doing keyword analysis:

Free

- Google Trends
- Answer the public
- Search Console

paid

- keywordtool.io
- semrush
- ahrefs

If you have 404 errors, fix them as soon as possible

HAVE YOU EVER CLICKED on a broken link? It's frustrating if you wanted to read some kind of information and you can't because the link is broken. But since you've been left with the desire, you search on Google and **end up reading the information on another site** .

404 errors not only "steal" potential readers, **they also make search engines take you less into account** for their rankings. They also do not like to invest their resources in pages that are not taken care of.

404 errors can occur for a number of reasons. Here we tell you some and how to fix them:

- If the content has been deleted and no longer exists, you apply a **410 redirect** to the url that no longer exists.
- If you have modified both the content and the url, and the new content is similar to the old, you can apply a **301 redirect** .
- If the 404 error is for a page that you have deleted by mistake, it would be enough to restore it and **leave the url as at the beginning** .
- sometimes the error is because you have put the wrong link. Just **check that it's spelled correctly** and it should be fixed.

When you're done fixing everything, remember to check again to confirm that everything is fixed.

So that you can get down to work, you can use this simple tool that identifies if you have 404 errors: Dead Link Checker

Image optimization for SEO

IMAGE OPTIMIZATION for SEO is an **essential practice** for any website that wants to improve its ranking in search results. Images can increase website traffic in a number of ways, so it's important to make sure they're optimized for search engines.

Here are some ideas for optimizing your site's images for SEO:

- Use alt text to describe images, as most search engines use this text to index them
- Write a relevant title and caption for each photo, as these are also used to index images in search engines
- Right-click on any image and then click "Save As" to see the name of the image file. Make sure the file name includes relevant keywords before saving.
- Reduce the size and number of images used on your website. Large images negatively affect site load time, which could lower your SEO Rankings.

Generate quality and useful content for the user

SOME BLOGGERS MAKE the mistake of thinking that quality content means long content. Not necessarily. In fact, **many readers prefer short, snappy** content to long content that can be boring.

When it comes to generating quality content, it's important to keep your audience in mind. That means creating content that is not only useful and informative, but also interesting and engaging. After all, if your content is boring, your audience is likely to lose interest quickly.

Some tips for writing quality content:

- Use simple and direct language.
- Focus on quality, not quantity. It is better to publish less content, but that this content is really useful and interesting, than to publish more content that does not contribute anything.
- Be sure to proofread your content for spelling and grammar errors.

- Add emotion to your content. Try to write engaging and attractive, so that people can not resist reading it.

Content Ideas

Use friendly urls throughout the website

FRIENDLY URLS ARE THOSE that have a **clean, simple structure** , and are easy to read and remember. A friendly url should be as short as possible, containing the main keywords of the content. In addition, the ideal is that the words are separated by hyphens and that they do not contain numbers or other types of characters.

The importance of Optimizing subtitles (h2, h3)

THE IMPORTANCE OF OPTIMIZING subheadings (h2, h3) lies in the need to maintain a good level of SEO. This is a technique that, if applied correctly, can significantly improve the positioning of a website in Google search results.

Subheadings **are used to organize the content of a web page and make it easier to read** . They are also useful for search engines, as they allow them to better understand the content of the page. Headings and subheadings must be used effectively to optimize content and enhance the user experience.

Reviewing headings and subheadings with the Chrome Web Developer extension

Use internal linking on your website

INTERNAL LINKING IS an SEO strategy that consists of **linking your own web pages to each other** . This helps search engines better index your site and can also improve traffic and conversions. There are several ways to do internal linking, but the most effective strategy is to do it through the use of **anchors and keywords** .

The purpose of internal linking is to facilitate navigation between the different sections of the site and also improve search engine positioning. The key to achieving a good result with internal linking is to use an appropriate strategy and according to the needs of the website.

Link externally to authority sites

BY EXTERNALLY LINKING to authority websites, you are improving the quality of your site's content and giving your readers the opportunity to get more information from trusted sources. External links are also a good way to establish your site as a source of quality information, which can attract more readers and potentially increase traffic to your site.

Use the meta-description well

THE META-DESCRIPTION is an element of HTML coding that provides a brief and precise summary of a web page. Although meta descriptions do not have a direct impact on rankings, if used effectively, they can help increase CTR (click-through rate) and ultimately improve website traffic.

Some tips to improve the meta description:

- Use between 130 and 142 characters
- Create compelling copy that complements your page title. The ideal is to use the main keyword, generate curiosity in the user and introduce a call to action.
- Don't trick the user into clicking.
- Review the meta descriptions of your competition and create

one that is unique to differentiate yourself.

Sign up for business directories

REGISTERING YOUR COMPANY in directories will improve the SEO positioning of your company since you will **be generating links to your website** . You also **increase your authority** , since directories are highly reputable websites for search engines. Another advantage of directories is that you allow users who use them to find you.

There are plenty of free directories where you can sign up by creating a business profile. **Some even allow you to use keywords or add links** to the most important pages on your website. Here are 4 directories to get you started:

- hotfrog
- Yalwa
- europages
- Spaininfo

How much can SEO cost to position a company?

WITHIN SEO, AS YOU have seen **, many things can be optimized** and the cost will vary depending on how optimized your company's website is. A page in which the main details have been taken care of and simply needs a little push is not the same as working with an online store with hundreds of products, filters and categories or, for example, finding a website that on a technical level has many failures.

SEO to position companies can be a complex endeavor, but **it is worth investing resources to position your company well** .

10 Tips to increase the traffic of your blog or website

Good traffic is important for any blog or website. The best ways to get traffic for a blog are through search engines. Do you have a blog or do you have a website? and Even though you have good content and you can't get much traffic?

If you are facing the above problems then this article is for you, I will give you 10 killer tips to increase your blog traffic.

How can I increase my blog traffic from 200 to 2000 visitors within 45 days?

Well I think this is the question that most bloggers have on their mind. Some bloggers who are new and my friends have asked me how can I increase my traffic in the shortest possible time, and that's why I decided to share this post. Then I explain the steps I followed to get traffic for my blog.

Content is King

I HAVE ALWAYS BELIEVED that content is the king for web traffic, if you have good content, you will automatically get traffic, but if your articles do not get indexed in Google, this is a matter of time and I assure you that after you write your articles within a few hours or minutes it will appear in Google searches.

So, you have to work harder and harder to write good content for your blog and so that each time your pages are indexed faster by Google.

Register your blog in search engines

THIS IS VERY IMPORTANT, even if you have good content, if your blog is not registered in the search engines (click here to see how to register your website with Google) you will not appear in the searches that people perform. The most important thing as soon as you start your blog is to register with search engines.

Social media

YES! THIS MADE ME CLOSER to success as Facebook helped me get traffic to my new blog, I used to share my daily articles on Facebook groups without wasting a single day, within a month my traffic was always increasing. Twitter is also the net of the planet, sharing your articles surely the traffic of your web page will increase.

Use the right keywords

USING THE RIGHT KEYWORDS is very important to get search traffic. If you don't use good titles for your articles, how can visitors expect good content if the title isn't right?

Do keyword research for each article you create, using Google AdWords.

internal links

YOU HAVE TO BE ABLE to keep visitors on the blog, the easiest and most successful way is to link the related content of your blog. You can do the following to achieve visitor retention:

- Use links in the content to other posts on your blog.
- Write related content and article series
- Have a section of related articles on your blog

Description of the article

THE DESCRIPTION IS very important in the articles, because if your title only contains one keyword, in the description you can include as many as you want.

LinkBuilding

THE BEST WAY TO GET links to your website, is to write or name some other blogs related to your topic, if the blog owner thinks your blog is worth referencing, then you already have a link to your website. Remember that if you have quality content, people who come to your blog for some reference will surely become your loyal reader.

Have a good feedback system

A GOOD COMMENT SYSTEM always helps to get more and more comments, observations and comments will help people to participate and new visitors will see that your blog is popular and generates conversation.

SEO

SEO IS ALWAYS THE BEST way to get traffic through search engines like Google, Yahoo, Bing.

If you want more advice or have a question with SEO, write us in the comments area and I will contact you immediately.

Have a good design and self-control

YES! BLOG DESIGN PLAYS an important role in increasing traffic, if it is quality and easy to use, this makes the reader feel comfortable and therefore spends more time on your blog.

Domain: The selection of a domain is also very important.

5 Tips for Writing Irresistible Titles for Your Blog

The inspiration came to you and you are ready to write an article on your blog, what you always hope is that it will be a success and that many people will read it and comment on it.

The title shouldn't be the first step in your planning process, but usually most people automatically start thinking about the title they'll give the article they're creating.

What all bloggers want is a headline that draws crowds. Do you want one of those titles that gets readers excited before they've even opened your article?

8 out of 10 readers on average will read only the title of the article, while less than 3 out of 10 readers will read the rest of the article. This is a simple statistic that shows how the post title greatly affects all content.

In order to quickly get the reader's attention, you need to find clever ways to write headlines that engage readers.

Imagine a reader typing a few keywords into the Google search engine. Google returns a list of search results and your title appears in the first list of results. What do you think the reader does first?

It's very simple. He or she will scan through the list and choose the best title. Based on my experience here are 5 tips that will help you write headlines that readers won't be able to resist and will end up clicking through to read the full article.

1. Put Passion

REMEMBER THAT SEARCH engines are not the primary audience you write for, so it's important to put some passion into your article titles.

I put passion in this list of tips first, as it can determine how readers open the article you've published.

You can't do well at something without love and passion, the same applies when you blog. The only way to bring a post title to life is to let passion take control of your writing. When there is passion, every part necessary to write a good title will sooner or later come to light.

2. Keep it short but precise

THE REASON TO WRITE an article on a blog is that more and more people read it. Certain?

To help connect readers to your blog, you need your article titles to clearly explain what the message is about. The era of super long titles is over. When writing your article title, try to keep it short, but also informative and compelling.

These two titles can give you an idea of what I'm talking about:

"5 Tips to Write Irresistible Titles for Your Blog" this title is much better compared to "Writing an Ad Title: Top 5 Tips on How to Write a Headline for Your Web Contents and Get High Attention".

3. Strike a balance in the keywords you use in the title of your post

WHEN IT COMES TO THINKING about SEO, using keywords in your blog title is highly recommended, but it's important not to overdo it. Article titles should be eye-catching, meaningful, and easy to read, so don't try to cram useless words into your title.

Regarding the two titles that I mention in point two, the first title has nine words, while the second has 18. In most cases, placing titles with 10 words or less and containing at least 2 keywords, In **SEO** it is considered very good and will help both in the ranking and attract the attention of readers.

4. Good grammar

JUST BECAUSE SEARCH engines don't care about grammar doesn't mean your articles shouldn't have good grammar. Nowadays, all the readers want to read well structured blogs, which includes good grammar.

It becomes even more important when you are writing the title of the article, because that is the first thing the reader sees and what helps them decide whether to continue reading the rest of the post.

More than once I have skipped an article, because the title is badly created. If you don't pay attention to grammar, you never know how many readers will stop clicking because they don't understand what your post is about.

5. Be careful when using special characters in titles

THERE ARE MANY SPECIAL characters that can be used in post titles.

The following special characters can be used in your titles: hyphen (-), colon (:), question mark (?), exclamation point ()!!

- The hyphen (-) can be used to separate words in the title
- The colon (:) like the hyphen, can be used to separate words in titles
- The question mark (?) when the title itself, is a question.
- The exclamation point (!), This character is used when the title is intended to make the reader emotional.

The following special characters are not recommended for use in titles: ampersand (&), greater than and less than symbol (<y>), number sign (#), at sign (@).

BOTTOM LINE: THERE is no single correct way to write blog titles. However, learning how to write and tips like these will help us stay ten steps ahead of our competitors.

5 free SEO tools that will help check your web traffic

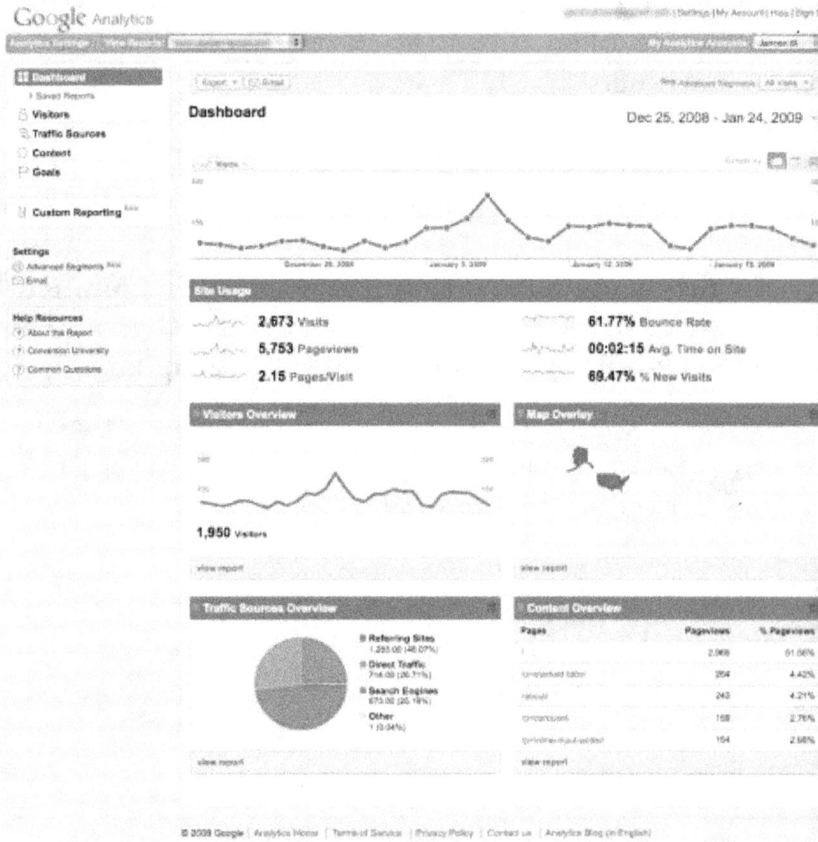

SEO tools are an integral part of the success of any website. If you want to know the state in which your website is and you want to give it a boost in the ranking, these tools are what you need and also I tell you something good, they are free.

There are a few bloggers who have disagreed with this and have said that it only takes your mind to improve your web ranking, but then again, their blogs are also on page 1000 of any site ranking, so we all need a little help

You don't have to spend a lot of money on SEO tools, in fact for the ones I'm presenting to you today you don't have to spend anything. Below is a list of our favorite SEO tools that you can use to help give your website a website ranking boost.

1. Google Adwords

WHEN IT COMES TO SEO, we cannot fail to mention Google Adwords. What I really like about this tool is its keyword finding feature. With this tool you can know exactly which keywords are hot and which are not. You can also enter your own keyword or some keyword phrase and you will see all the results that it will show you. A list of the competition, global monthly searches, and monthly local searches will appear so you can get an idea of how successful any given keyword is and decide which one you want to use on your website or blog.

2. SEOmoz

THIS TOOL IS THE BEST tool for anyone who is cautious about Google and does not allow their website access to it. SEOmoz allows you to check the daily ranking for up to 5 different keywords for free (which add up to 150 words per month). It also maintains an archive, which will allow you to better track and monitor your website or blog's success.

The tool has to be good as big companies like Disney and Best Buy are using it. It is credited for being one of the most comprehensive and comprehensive SEO tools on the web.

3. Multirank Checker

CREATED BY IWEBTOOL.com, there really isn't a rank check tool that is easier than this tool. If you are interested in testing the ranking of your page in Google or Bing, all you have to do is put your domain name or names in the text field.

That's right, you can review all your domains and not have to go through each unique domain name. That alone can be a huge time saver if you have multiple sites on the web. You receive a results table at the end that you can copy and paste and save for future reference.

4. Fiddler the Fiddler

YOU CAN USE THE FREE app, Fiddler, first to debug your site. Fiddler works in such a way that it is able to capture all HTTP traffic coming through your site and it will be logged for review. It is also capable of "tinkering" with HTTP traffic that is new to your website.

The most recent version of Fiddler, Fiddler2, goes further and now offers additional support for dealing with HTTPS traffic. It, too, is a free download that can be easily found on the web and start using immediately.

5. Overture Keyword Selector Tool

OVERTURE KEYWORD SELECTOR Tool is a tool that can at least partially replace Google Adwords, if you are not a fan of Google. The good thing about Overture is that it is quite easy to use. This site, run by Yahoo!, only requires you to enter a keyword or keyword phrase and will then give you a list of other keywords that are more searchable and help you see how they rank.

For example, let's say you captured the keyword "web hosting ". The tool will give you a list of the top keyword searches related to the one you captured.

Local SEO Checklist for Small Business

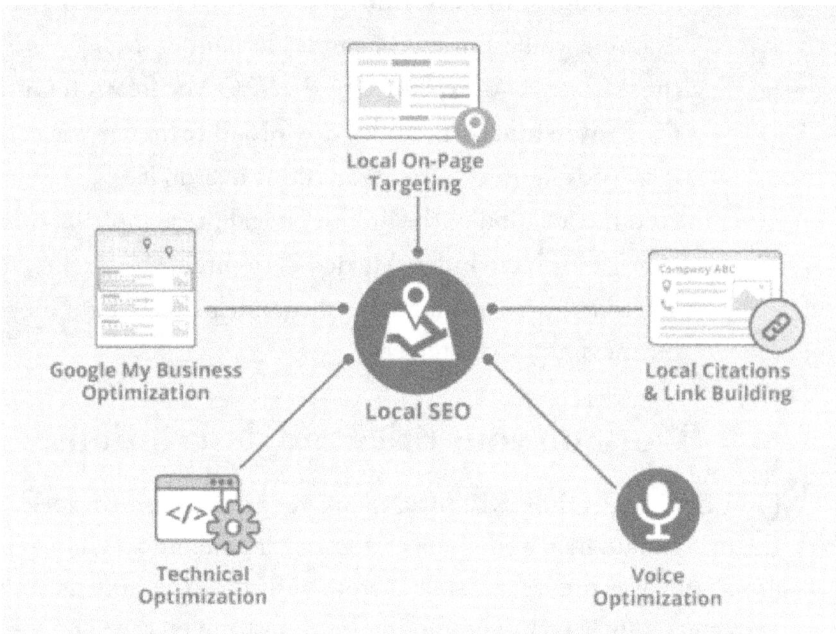

In the previous article I talked about the importance and benefits of local SEO for businesses, but in this post we will look at what you need to do in order to optimize your website for local search. Next we will see the local SEO checklist.

Optimize your logo.

One of the first things search engines find when crawling your website is your logo image and this is a good place to start your local SEO optimization.

- Make sure the image file name is descriptive. Instead of using logo.png, use a more meaningful description like 'abogados-hernandez-logo.png'

- Alt text is important for all images, but more important for the logo. You can use ALT text to give more details about the image and, in this case, the location of your business. For example, you can use "Abogados Hernández, México DF" for the ALT text. As explained in the **SEO Verification Guide for Professionals (includes download format)**, you can use keywords in the ALT text, but don't overdo it.
- Add the location in the link title tag. For example <a title = "Abogados Hernández, Mexico City" href = ".... </ a>
- Try to use the same logo on all channels (Web, FB, Google+ business page, Twitter, etc.)

Work on your titles and descriptions.

TITLES AND DESCRIPTIONS are very important for local SEO. The title should help both users and search engines understand as much about the website as possible before visiting. The title is only 70 characters, but if you are targeting local customers, then the location (and if possible the phone number) should be part of your title and description. A couple of real examples from the web:

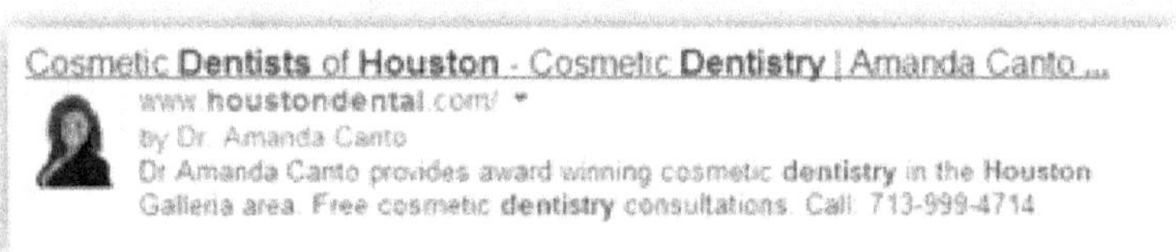

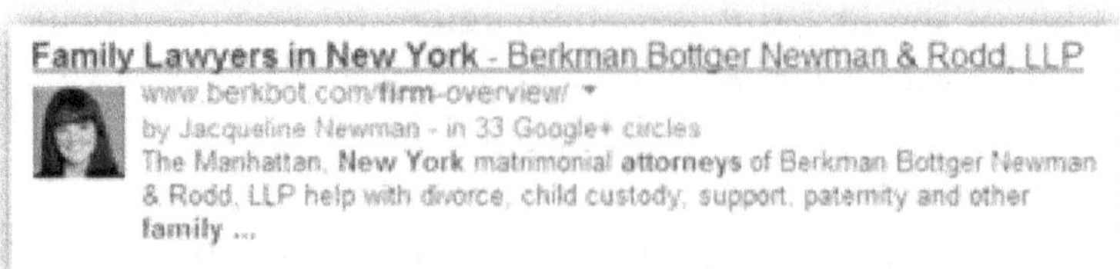

All address details and contact information on the front page.

ON THE MAIN PAGE YOU must ensure that your full address details (street and number, postal code, state, country, telephone number, fax number, email) are visible in text form (not image) in a prominent position on the home page. You can add this information in the sidebar, for example.

Full address details and contact information for the rest of the pages.

THE REST OF THE PAGES should have the contact information in the footer (if you don't want to keep it in the sidebar). I separated the home page from the rest of the pages to highlight the importance of contact information to be visible on the main page.

Add a map on the contact information page.

IT'S VERY EASY TO ADD a Google map of your business to the contact page and another indication of your location for search engines.

Create a Google+ Business Page.

MAKE SURE YOU FILL in your contact details and that these are the same as the contact information you have on your website, on FB and everywhere else. Be sure to provide enough information in the 'About' (including your location).

Sign up for Google Places for Business.

GOOGLE WILL VERIFY your address and business ownership and then get to respond to customer feedback and provide more information about your business.

Implement Google Authorship.

THIS DOESN'T HAVE A direct impact on local SEO, but it can help get more hits once it shows up in search results. Several studies have shown that users are more likely to click on a link that displays its author along with the page title and description.

Use markup structured data to give more information about your local Google business.

WHEN YOU GO BACK INTO webmaster tools, under 'additional tools' you can find the 'Structured Markup Data Helper' tool. **You can use the local businesses** option to tell Google about your business name, location, etc. You can then download the file and add it to your web page.

Sign up for Bing Places.

BING PLACES for Business is free, easy to fill out, and another way to verify your business information online. Don't forget to link to your Bing profile from your Google+ business page.

Register in local directories.

LIST YOUR BUSINESSES to trusted local directories and remember to be consistent in the address details you are using. You don't have to overdo it, but just submit your businesses to quality local directories.

Create a Facebook business page.

IN ADDITION TO PROVIDING other information you also need to make sure that the address and phone number are filled out correctly. Once you are done going in and editing your Google+ business page you must add a link to your FB business page.

List your business with Yelp for Business . Yelp for Business

IT'S FREE AND EASY to set up. Once you complete your profile put a link on your page

Register with Foursquare for Business

- **FOURSQUARE FOR BUSINESS** is another directory to use to enforce your local SEO efforts. With more than 40 million registered users and the increasing use of mobile phones, it is worth taking the time and effort to maintain your list of businesses with them.

Encourage and respond to every comment on all platforms .

IN ADDITION TO YOUR registration on the above platforms, it is important to encourage users to review your business and it is equally important to respond to all comments (good or bad). By answering this you will encourage more users to leave comments.

You can also ask your customers to leave a comment.

THIS ON THEIR FAVORITE platform either by giving them incentives ie 5% on their next purchase or by sending SMS or email reminders.

Mentions in the local press.

IT HELPS PEOPLE WHO don't know it to know where it is located and what its page is on the internet.

SEO Audit.

AS MENTIONED ABOVE traditional SEO is still important so it is best to carry out an SEO audit of your website for compliance with standards and best practices.

Mobile optimization.

DON'T FORGET ABOUT mobile, especially when it comes to finding customers locally.

Start a blog .

How can a blog help in local SEO?

YOU CAN POST HIGH-QUALITY content regularly and build internal links. For example from a blog post you can link to your services pages by "financial services in Mexico". This alone is not going to do much, but it is a small step in your overall optimization process.

You can also use the blog for the use of local keywords in the title and content of blog posts

Twitter, Pinterest, YouTube and more.

I HAVEN'T MENTIONED Twitter, Pinterest, Youtube or other social networks separately, but for best results, you also have to keep an exact profile of those as well. These networks are also great for getting leads.

Can you perform local SEO with PPC?

ONE OF THE MOST FREQUENTLY asked questions I get when talking to clients about their local SEO strategy is whether you can use targeted PPC campaigns and get local customers instead of trying to get customers through organic search.

The answer is simple and straightforward, yes you can use PPC to bring local customers.

Conclusion

LOCAL SEO IS A VALUABLE tool for every business that has a physical address and wants to use the Internet to get more customers for their business/services/products in their area.

The techniques to use for local SEO are on top of traditional SEO techniques which means you should first do your SEO as you would regardless of local and then optimize using the methods outlined above.

In a nutshell, the most important aspects of local SEO are:

- View contact information on your website
- Use the same consistent address everywhere
- Sign up for Google+ for business, FB and other directories
- Try to get people to comment on your business on trusted services and make sure that every comment gets a response.

PPC and SEO: The Dynamic Duo

ONLINE MARKETING AGENCIES must use both PPC (pay per click) and SEO tactics in order to get the most out of their search marketing campaigns.

In search engine marketing, pay per click and search engine optimization (SEO) each have their own complexities to improve performance. Focusing on those complexities can achieve some great benefits, which helps us get better performance as long as you look at and work with the similarities of both channels.

The obvious similarity is that both channels drive traffic through keywords. The most important similarity is that both channels strive to match the intent of the user and the content of the page being promoted. The knowledge gained from this fight is the commonality that can make both channels a dynamic duo.

One of the biggest differences between the two channels is timing. PPC can provide instant results while SEO can take a long period of time to achieve results. The time advantage that PPC ultimately has can provide great insights into what can be developed over time in SEO. You can rely on the following points

- Use different keywords in your PPC strategy

- Use the same keywords of your PPC strategy in SEO
- Create different titles for your PPC ads
- Use the titles of your PPC ads in the articles you post on your blog.
- Having more published articles gives your PPC strategy more landing pages.

The need for content creation in SEO gives your PPC strategy more landing pages to satisfy user intent. Learning what content is most effective through SEO can provide PPC with new avenues for growth.

Sometimes there are PPC campaigns that are not generating results, so they are forgotten. But SEO is always on and metrics that once provided poor PPC results can change at any moment. Make sure you are monitoring your SEO content metrics to determine when those changes occur. Seasonality is a great example; Changes in content metrics via SEO can signal that PPC campaigns need to get going.

There is also evidence showing the presence of both a paid search and an organic listing can be mutually beneficial. Imagine that your business appearing in both paid and organic results can be an indicator of a user's trust. You can also take advantage of driving a user to your website through cross-channel messaging. You can rank first organically for a phrase and for a keyword using paid results, that would be great don't you think.

Competition can be fierce on websites, so we need to take advantage of every opportunity.

The benefits of sharing strategies between PPC and SEO are very significant and could ultimately mean the difference between winning or losing.

Have you launched any SEO campaign or strategy, what were its results? And what do you think of SEO and PPC?

Google SEO best practices - how to keep Google happy

• • • •

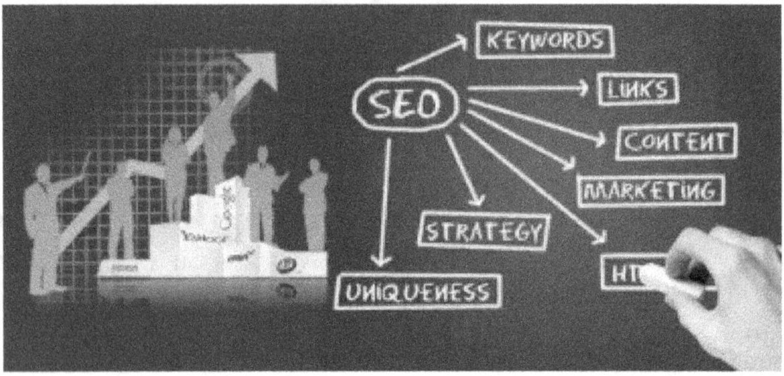

IN THIS ARTICLE WE will look at SEO best practices that will help you keep both users and Google happy. Find out what you need to do to earn the respect and love of the world's largest search engine.

So without all the fuss, what's the secret formula to get 1 million Google hits and how can you make sure your website uses the best SEO practices to keep Google and your visitors happy?

1. Original and unique content

LET'S REMEMBER THAT **content is always king** . I don't know how many times in the last 13 years, I've read this phrase "original and unique content or content is king", I'm not sure how many thousands of times I've told myself. It's becoming a cliché, but yeah If you want to have any chance of getting traffic from Google you need to have high quality, original and unique content published on your website.

2. Participatory content

PUBLISHING ORIGINAL and unique content is the first step, but it's not enough. Your content has to stand out and the only way to do that is through user engagement. By user participation we mean comments on the site, likes, Google+, tweets, etc.

Why is this important?

TO BEGIN WITH, IT IS clear that social signals (comments are a social signal too) have begun to play a more important role when it comes to ranking in Google and to delve deeper into the subject, check out the following example.

Two web pages on the same topic, but on different websites, compete for one of the top positions in Google for a certain keyword. One of the pages has 30 comments, 100 likes and 42 tweets and the other page has no comments or social media mentions.

All things being equal, which page deserves a better ranking? I think the answer is pretty obvious and the reasoning behind it is that user engagement is a signal that the particular page is important to users. What do you think?

Since search engines want to include web pages in their results that help users, the page that has been shown (through user input) to be most important is more likely to be selected.

3. Good titles and descriptions

IF THERE IS ONE THING that Google mentions whenever SEO is discussed, it is the importance of having good titles and descriptions. I don't have more details and examples in my SEO Tips article but the general guidelines are:

- Titles must be less than 70 characters in length
- Descriptions must be less than 160 characters

- Titles and descriptions must be unique for each page on your website
- If you want your customers to be from a specific country, then optimize both your titles and descriptions for local SEO

4. Show your expertise

THIS IS AGAIN RELATED to the quality of the content, but if you are an expert on a subject, be sure to show it on your website. Google is looking for trusted sources and if your professional experience or knowledge on a subject you do, you have to show it on your website.

You also need to understand that the web is no longer anonymous so you need to show who you are, what you do and so that your readers / customers / followers can trust you. If you can convince people to trust you, Google (and other search engines) will trust you too.

5. 100% Compatibility When It Comes to On-Page SEO

ON-PAGE SEO OPTIMIZATION is a term that describes everything that needs to be done on the website itself so that it is optimized for search engines. It is not difficult to have an SEO optimized website and it is the first check that you have to do when evaluating the presence of the Internet in general.

In the article **SEO verification guide for professionals (includes download format**) you can verify all the points that you must take into account on the page. It includes a download format which is a checklist that helps you carry out this activity.

I consider that on-page SEO is more important every day and that is why I suggested that it has to be 100% compatible. You should check that your website's on-page SEO techniques are in good condition before doing any type of promotion.

6. Never Violate Google's Webmaster Guidelines

ALTHOUGH GOOGLE IS trying to give webmasters feedback when their guidelines are violated (through webmaster tools) so that they can take corrective action, it's best not to violate their guidelines in the first place.

From my experience, violation of the guidelines can happen when you are not familiar with the guidelines and because you don't know them you can violate them without knowing it and second you know that you are violating the guidelines, but you are doing it with the belief that this way you will get more traffic and faster results.

Another thing that can happen is that you hire an SEO expert and he is offering you the moon, the sun and the stars and you are actually violating Google's policies. You can review the article **5 Things an SEO consultant will never tell you** to know how to deal with an SEO expert.

7. Keep your website fresh

GOOGLE LOVES FRESH content and up-to-date websites. Give Google one more reason to differentiate your website from the competition by delivering high-quality content on a regular basis.

How often should you update your website? It depends on the **market niche, the competition and the type of content** . For example, if you have a technology website, you need to have opinions on the latest equipment, to show Google that you are in tune with the latest updates in your niche.

8. Stay in tune with the latest trends

ONE OF THE WAYS TO get the most out of SEO for Google is to stay in tune with the latest developments. The Google quality team periodically makes changes to its algorithm and you have to follow their steps to avoid unpleasant surprises.

For example, the latest SEO trends this period (until October 2013) are attention to websites for mobile phones, Google authoring and Google + for business. Plus updates on Penguin, Panda and the release of Hummingbird.

If you want to make sure that your website is up to date, you will have to keep an eye on what's new in the market.

Lastly, is Google SEO different than Bing SEO?

When we talk about organic traffic and SEO we always refer to Google and we forget about search engines like Bing or others. The truth is that without Google, it is very difficult to succeed online.

When it comes to Bing we don't worry as much because the same rules that apply for Google SEO apply there. They have even recently updated their guidelines mentioning that excessive link building can lead to your website being removed from search listings.

Conclusion

THE CONCLUSION OF THIS article is simple: if you want to dominate Google SEO and keep the search giant happy so that you get visitors from the search results, you have to play by the rules.

Forget easy tricks or black hat practices, close your eyes and ears to those who want to believe that there is a magical way to bypass Google algorithms and start thinking about how you can create a website that has something to offer to visitors and have value.

When you manage to create a website that stands out, you can be sure that traffic from Google will start flowing with or without SEO.

50 Questions and Answers about SEO and search engine positioning

50 Questions about SEO as you have written in Google

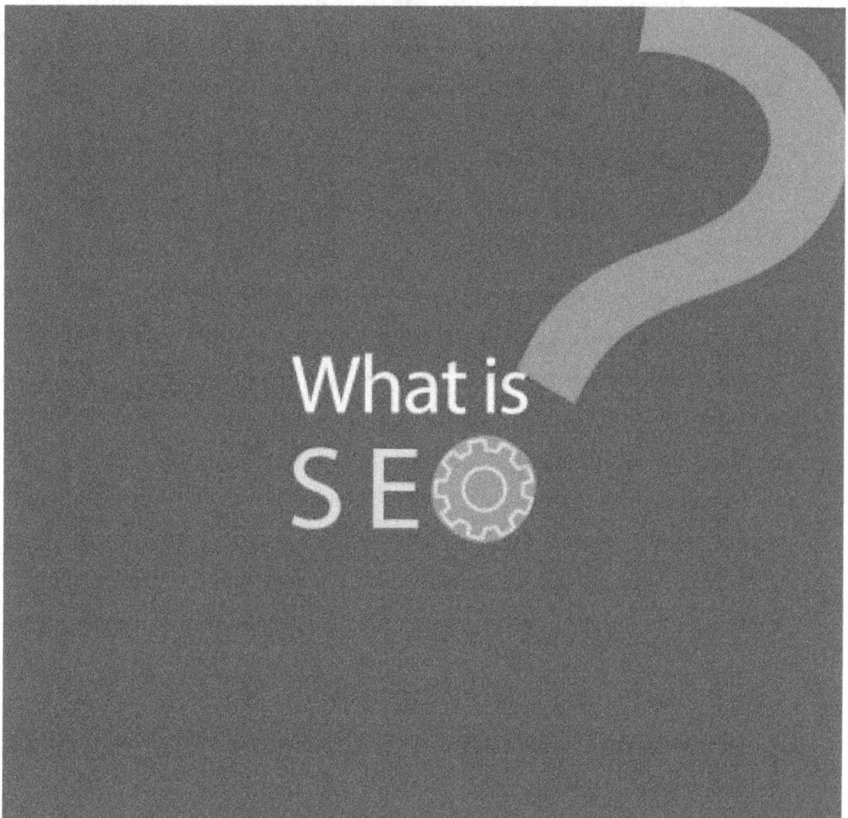

••••

1. Is it good for website SEO to put comments?

IT IS VERY GOOD FOR any page or blog to have comments enabled, at least in the newsfeed or blog. Comments keep your site updated constantly and Google sees you and ranks you as a page with continuous activity.

Perhaps you are worried that the **keyword density of** your page will be blurred by the new words in the comments. I would not worry much because search engines take more into account the first words. You can use some trick to maintain a similar density of words:

- **Do not repeat** the same words a lot that are not your Keywords; for example: Thank you. You will use different words to thank the participation so that Google does not think that your article is about Thank you.
- **Use your keywords** in the comments and take the opportunity to use new phrases and terms that could result in some search and search engine visits.

In addition, comments are essential to be able to connect with the reader and exercise two-way communication 2.0. You should use your page not only to tell, but also to listen and participate. I give you the same advice as a reader: comment and share all the interesting articles you read.

2. Five things you can do so that your web page has a good positioning

THIS HAS AMUSED ME. He is not looking for 4 or 6, he wants 5 things to have good SEO. It is difficult to choose and summarize only five things so that your page has a good search engine position, but I am going to try.

- **Choose your keywords well.** The first step is essential, because you could rank first for keywords that do not give you any results or profitability. First you must know how many times each term is searched, for example with Google Trends . If you also want to know the competition for each search, use this Google Adwords tool . The second step is to study the conversion of each keyword to find out which ones give you the highest profitability. We would use Google Analytics .

- **Use your keywords well.** You will use them to create your titles, you will repeat them in your articles, you will put them in bold from time to time...
- **Get good links to your pages.** Search engines understand the links to your site as recommendations, therefore the websites with the most and best recommendations will appear in the first results. The best technique to get quality links is to create great and ambitious content. Also the links obtained in social networks are of great importance.
- **Take care of the loading speed of your pages.** It is another of the most important factors since Google is determined to offer us the best possible experience on the Internet. You can use the Gt Metrix tool and check out my 75 Steps to SEO to see what you can improve.
- **Good setup of the site and posts.** Provides titles and descriptions for images; use Google Webmaster Tools to set up your page; edit a different title and Meta description for each page and study the conversion of each one; avoid duplicate content; adapt your website to all mobile devices; avoid Google penalties...

3. Create a website that can be seen on mobile devices

IT IS IMPORTANT FOR your positioning that visitors remain on your page for as long as possible. If your website does not look correctly on mobile phones and tablets, the average stay time and usability will drop a lot.

You can use a **Responsive design** or adapt your current design to be responsive. The Responsive or Adaptable design is nothing more than telling your website how you want it to look for different resolutions. With a few new lines of code in your CSS you can make any website Responsive. If you are looking for someone to help you with this, here I am. Check how your page looks on mobile .

4. How long does it take to improve my All in One SEO Pack page?

ALL IN ONE SEO PACK IS a WordPress plugin that I recommend. In any case, it is only a tool that we must use and configure to obtain results. Do not expect that just by installing the plugin your website will jump to the top positions. With it you will have to edit and refine a title and description for each of your pages.

If you have already worked on it a lot, when will you notice the changes? Well, very quickly, in two days. You will see at least that your results in Google already come out with a different title and description.

5. How many SEOs can wordpress have?

THIS QUESTION ALSO amused me and I am going to have to interpret a little what it means. It is likely referring to the number **of SEO plugins** a WordPress blog can have. If they are generic SEO plugins with many functions, we can only have one. You will have to choose, for example, between All in One SEO Pack or SEO by Yoast .

Other small plugins with exclusive functionalities if we can complement them with another generic one. Some templates include SEO functions and most of the time it is possible and advisable to disable them if we use an SEO plugin with the same functions.

6. Where to put the javascript code to improve web positioning?

THE JAVASCRIPT IS ONE of the things that weighs the most on our website. Search engines appreciate that java is loaded late in the process, so visitors don't have to wait for it to load. It would be advisable that the code be loaded through a **JS file** and not written directly in the Html.

To make the call to load that file, it would be best to put it as low as possible in your Html. Depending on the type of functions, sometimes it may be at the end of the *BODY* and sometimes at the end of the *HEAD* .

7. SEO tool to see what people are asking about a topic

SOMETIMES WE TRY TO look for very complicated tools when the best one is almost always **Google** . In this case, with Twitter you will also be able to know thousands of concerns about any topic. If what you want to know is the amount, what they ask the most and what they ask the least, then use Google Trends .

8. Do the colors of a website matter for positioning in Google?

NICE, A SHORT ONE! NOT.

9. Illegal ways to position your page first of all

WELL, LOOK, I'M GOING to save this one too, because I don't think it's very educational or that it takes me anywhere to explain things like this. Some malice and anecdote have ever escaped me with my students. Also don't think there is any method that won't backfire when Google catches you. **The cheap and easy in SEO is expensive** .

10. Page to automatically detect if there is good SEO

AGAIN GOOGLE IS GOING to tell us everything. Enter your keywords in Google search and see the results. If you appear on the first pages, you have good SEO. If you want to evaluate your website in different aspects of SEO and suggest possible improvements, use for example Woorank .

11. Steps to put a page in a search engine

YOUR PAGES WILL APPEAR in the search engines when another page that already appears in Google links you. If you want to shorten this step, you can directly submit your URL to Google .

12. Who makes the sitemap, the programmer or the SEO?

ANYONE BECAUSE IT SUCKS. In 1 minute for example with XML-Sitemaps .

13. Loss of position in some keywords by increasing links to others

IT IS POSSIBLE THAT you lose positions in certain keywords if you work on others from a different area and Google classifies you in another category. I think it is more common that something else is happening to you. Maybe you used dubious techniques to get the new links and **Google is penalizing you** .

14. Where to hire SEO?

HEY!! WHERE DID YOU go!! I see that the visitor who searched for this spent 9 minutes and 36 seconds reading my 75-Step Guide to SEO . I don't know if in the end he learned enough to do the SEO himself. If you have not been good at it, I will give you an SEO budget without obligation . You if you want too.

15. Plugins to improve search engine positioning

I HAVE ALREADY TOLD you about All in One SEO Pack and I can also recommend: Seo by Yoast, W3 Total Cache, XML Sitemaps, JS & CSS Optimizer, P3 Performer, SEO Rank Reporter...

16. What does the SEO of your website mean?

WE COULD DEFINE IT as the set of actions that we can carry out to improve the natural positioning in search engines.

17. SEO rules at the time of making a website

IF YOU ARE GOING TO start a website from the beginning you can take into account two important things:

- **Speed:** That the template and design do not need a lot of loading time.
- **Responsive:** That the design is adaptable for mobile phones and tablets.

18. SEO, what happens if the posts are deleted?

IF A POST IS DELETED, it will also immediately **disappear** from Google results and all the positioning that it could generate for you. What you can do is create a page with the same URL and content that the post had. If you don't link to this page on your website, it will be invisible to your other visitors, but it will still receive visits from Google.

19. Is it useful to repeat words to be better positioned in Google?

WELL, EVEN IF IT SEEMS very basic and very silly: Yes. As long as it is natural and without going too far.

20. Time needed to rank on Google

TO APPEAR ON GOOGLE you need 1 day. To position yourself well is something else, it can take a lifetime and not get it. Like everything, **it depends on the competition** you have. If you do things right and get natural recommendations from other websites, in 1 or 2 months you should have already noticed great results.

21. Does Cloudflare benefit SEO?

CLOUDFLARE IS A CDN and therefore benefits SEO in several ways. CDNs actually get the visitor into a parallel copy of your blog hosted on a secure third-party server.

22. How to do SEO with two words?

I UNDERSTAND THAT YOU intend to position a keyword made up of two words. The shorter your keywords are, the more competition you will have to position them. The **Long Tail** theory shows us that it would be convenient to try to position different combinations of those words with others.

To give you an example: it will be very difficult to position "buy a car", and it will be easier and more profitable for you to work on the SEO of "buy a cheap car in Madrid", "buy a car that consumes little", "buy a discount car in Madrid"...

23. How to position yourself SEO for real?

THIS HAS DELIGHTED me. She spent over 13 minutes reading the 75 Steps to SEO, so I hope she didn't find it fake SEO.

SEO does what it does, and well done, it gives **guaranteed results** . Of course, we cannot expect miraculous results out of context. A good SEO job can ensure you come out first for certain searches. If those searches don't have enough volume and you don't convert well... then you might mistakenly think it was fake SEO.

24. Free SEO Tools

THERE ARE ZILLIONS of thousands. I'll write an article soon showing you how to use my favorites, but for now I'm going to give you this small collection of the ones I remember right now: Internet Marketing Ninjas , Woorank , Google Adwords Keyword , Cute Rank , Raven SEO tools , Sheer SEO , WebCeo , Nibbler , Authority Labs , SEOChat SEO Tools , SeoMoz , GtMetrix , SEO Book , Screaming Frog ...

25. What is the future of SEO?

THE FUTURE OF SEO IS going to be with a **greater demand** and with **subspecializations** in different fields. Some already tell me that the SEO that I explain is SEO Off Page and that now it is no longer considered SEO but WPO (Web Performance Optimization). Well very good! And there is also the SMO (Social Media Optimization), the GEO SEO and more that will come out.

26. How to improve search engine positioning with Google+?

WITH GOOGLE+ YOU CAN post with a personal profile or with a page profile, similar to Facebook. All the links to your site will help to position you, as well as the popularity that the publications and shares could have.

Likewise , **your links are being shared** on Google+ by other people if you promote it from your blog. As you do in other social networks, it is a good strategy to search for them and comment on them to help them have more visibility. You have to use Google+ NOW if you are not doing it, and participate with those who share your content if you want to position yourself in Google's favorite social network. You can start by following me on Google+ and mentioning me when you share something interesting. If it is really useful I will comment and I will +1.

27. Does an SEO need to know how to program?

LET'S SEE, PROGRAMMING sounds very serious, but "programming" in **Html and Css** can be learned in 4 afternoons. I understand that if it is necessary for an SEO to know the basics and be able to understand the files. SEO works with the ins and outs of the Web and it would be a huge disadvantage not to speak the language. I recommend learning the basics because you could do a lot better like SEO with them.

28. How to find illegal SEO?

I SUPPOSE YOU MEAN how to know if your website has **illegal SEO positioning** , and therefore you have lost or are going to lose all your visits with Google penalties. This is the easiest way to know if the positioning of a website is of dubious arts. Look for the address of that website in quotes and see if it has hundreds or thousands of links with the same anchor text in foreign directories, low-quality websites or meaningless platforms.

29. How to know if they do the web positioning well?

HOW OTHERS ARE DOING SEO for you is easy to check. You will have reached an agreement on the searches you want to position and a compromise of results. Do that search in Google and if you come out first or in the position that you would have agreed, then the SEO has done you well. If you are looking for generic data you can use WooRank .

30. How to use blogs to improve the SEO of your website?

VERY EASY: **Publishing valuable content** about your keywords and your market areas. There are millions of people asking questions on Google and you have the opportunity to help them and have them visit you to find that information. Good content will give you inbound links and help you rank for many different searches.

31. Where to put links for SEO?

THIS IS ONE OF THE most repeated searches and I have received it in many different ways. A few years ago I also went crazy finding sites to link to my website, but believe that it is not everything in SEO. Generally the crazy link forgets many other things that would give better results. Still I tell you **where to put links** :

- Current directories and those of your sector
- Forums and discussion groups in which you participate. Spam no.
- Solve doubts and questions that people ask on the internet. Search with Google.
- Register in all the social networks and tools, to study them... and to put your links.
- Social media posts from you and others are also links to your

website

- News aggregators such as Meneame, MktFan, Digg, Reedit, Bitacoras, Globedia...
- Comment and participate in blogs in your community. Have you tried helping the blog owner answer all his comments? I assure you that you earn it and it links you in an article.

32. Pages to practice with Google Analytics

IT IS TRUE THAT FOR beginners it can be difficult to practice **Google Analytics** if you do not have a blog hosted on your own server or hosting. I solve this problem with Tumblr in the Aula CM Community Manager Course and the students test the Tumblr micro-blogs while practicing with Google Analytics.

33. Is Html good or bad for SEO?

COOL! **Html** is the language in which all web pages are written. Google values a clean, fast and correct Html, and if you work on positioning you should also value it and at least understand it. If you want to know if the Html of your page complies with the standards, you can use the W3 Markup Validator .

34. Is it bad to have SEO 2 times at the same time?

IT IS BAD TO HAVE 2 SEO plugins that do the same functions. If you mean if you can have two SEO workers... there is no problem as long as they get along and know how to work as a team.

35. Is SEO good to have links to other websites?

ON THE ONE HAND, WE always **share our authority** when we link to other websites. If we have many links to other pages, it could happen that we share our positioning with them too much. But on the other hand, Google appreciates that we offer valuable resources on our pages, and classifies as interesting content if we share valued and well-positioned articles or sources of information.

What we have to be very careful about is checking these links from time to time. It is normal for you to have a broken link on your website and you have to be quick to correct them. You can use Internet Marketing Ninja Broken Links to discover broken links.

36. Make a page for each city for SEO

IT CAN BE A STRATEGY to follow to position your content for different locations and work from different pages on **Local SEO** . It can be very laborious to do the same positioning work for many similar websites, so you can also do it within the same page with subdomains or different categories by cities.

37. When I change from Joomla to WordPress I lose positioning

WHEN IT COMES TO CHANGING our publishing platform, it is very normal to lose part of the positioning we had. Google will have to **reindex** our entire site and as much as we put in the old content, most of it will be different. You can try to replicate as much as possible your previous page in the new one. Copy the same articles and pages that you had and try to have the same URL as before. Also check the incoming links so there are no broken ones.

38. Is it good to buy SEO links?

THERE IS A HOAX THAT says that if you buy links you will be **penalized by Google** . It's only possible to find out if you buy link packs, which I advise against for everyone. Generally these 100, 500 or 1000 links are from low quality directories that give Google clues that we are trying to get links in an unnatural way.

What you can do is make a proposal to any page in your sector to link you permanently or in an article. If it is a page that does not usually do it in a shameless way, the search engines will never be able to know it. Good **SEO campaigns** with a certain budget usually have the purchase of links and mentions in leading blogs in the sector.

39. More text or more images for positioning?

IF YOU HAVE TO CHOOSE, more text. Remember to edit a title and a description for each image, since Google is the only thing that will understand it. It is convenient that you use at least one different image for each page, and that you try to position it individually with Pinterest and other pages where you can link it.

40. Best SEO site to write articles

IF YOU MEAN WHICH BLOGS you can write as **a guest author** : Puromarketing is one of the best that does it openly in Spanish. You can still propose it to many other blogs. If you want to write SEO articles and you don't have a blog, you can also write in Linkedin groups, but I recommend that you create a blog and put what you know into practice.

41. Perfect Template for SEO

YOU MUST CONFIGURE and tune the template you use to get the most out of SEO. Your choice is very important since there are things that will be very difficult to change later. There are two types of templates: some loaded with effects and cool, and others simpler. If we intend to do a **good positioning** with few resources, use one of the second.

Check the loading speed of each template and discover which ones offer you just what you need and are fast. With GtMetrix you can see what bugs they have, and if you're experienced you'll know which ones you can fix and which ones you can't. Once the template is chosen, try to remove the load of the expendable javascript, even if you lose some functionality.

42. Position a single keyword in SEO

POSITIONING A SINGLE word is the most difficult. The method is the same, but the competition is usually enormous. Try to use longer keywords that include this word, more or less following **the Long Tail Theory** .

43. What happened to Google in May 2013 SEO?

WELL, IT HAPPENED THAT **Google Penguin 2.0** (or Google Penguin 4) is about to arrive and it will be an **SEO Earthquake** . Google carried out some tests for 0.01% of the searches and the alarm went off. Stay tuned for the new Google Penguin update and prepare to lose thousands of visits... or gain them.

44. In SEO, 200 visits is little

MMMM... WELL, IT DEPENDS on what for, but yes, initially 200 visits is not enough, but everything is relative. If it were a commercial landing page, for which through ads you would pay €2 per visit... then 200 visits are something, exactly valued at €400.

45. Writing tips on web positioning and SEO

MY SUGGESTION IS THAT you try to write your **keywords** in the first 200 words. You can even make a lead at the beginning of each article summarizing it. Generally we look for synonyms so as not to repeat the same words, but in **SEO** it does not matter that you repeat your keywords from time to time.

It is useful to have a list of your keywords and different combinations and variations, to help you write your articles. You will see how some ideas and phrases come out alone when you think about your keywords.

46. Use several blogs to improve search engine positioning

I SUPPOSE YOU MEAN that to position a page you could create **many blogs** that give it incoming links. It seems to me a rather laborious strategy if we do not want it to be very artificial and Google catches you. It could be a recommended strategy if it is linked to a good Content Marketing strategy. The contents of the blogs would attract visitors who could be leads and show interest in our products.

47. Does learning SEO have a future?

I THINK A LOT. IT WILL be one of the most demanded professions in 2013 and 2014. Many professionals such as Community Managers and journalists have to learn some of these skills to get the most out of the web. Content **Marketing** or **Inbound Marketing** is going to mean a before and after for brands on the internet and SEO is a fundamental factor for Community Managers and Online Marketing specialists to take advantage of Content Marketing.

48. In a WordPress, where are the keywords placed for their positioning?

THEY ARE PLACED EVERYWHERE, especially in the titles and descriptions of each page. You can also write them in your articles, categories, tweets, image titles, videos, anchor texts...

• • • •

49. Improve positioning with an alternative text to the image

IT IS ESSENTIAL THAT you put a description and alternative text to all your images. If you have many without filling in, you can use a WordPress plugin that does it automatically with the title of the article: SEO Friendly Images .

50. Which pages are better to know about positioning?

THERE ARE MANY BETTER pages than mine to learn about search engine optimization, here I recommend one that I like: The greats blog of Matt Cutts , Search Engine Watch , SEOMoz , Distilled and Search Engine Land .

Natural referencing advantage and disadvantage

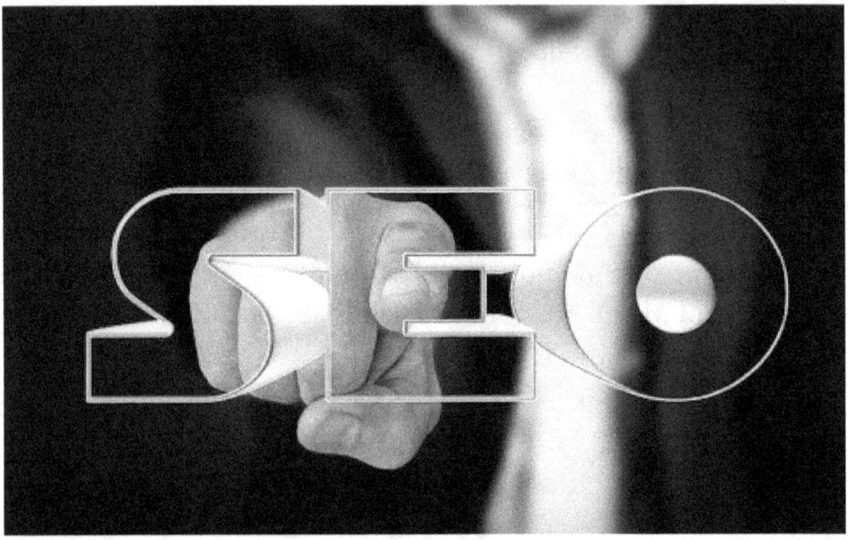

If you are in charge of your company's digital strategy, you know how important natural referencing or SEO is to improve the visibility of your website. Indeed, a good natural referencing strategy allows you to appear among the first results of the most popular search engines. However, is referencing your site with SEO really a good idea? What are the advantages and disadvantages of this mode of optimization?

What is the purpose of SEO work for your website?

FOR THE MARKETING STRATEGY to optimize your site to be a success, betting on natural referencing can be an alternative of choice. Indeed, you will be able to generate traffic on your site and obtain new customers thanks to seo referencing, in particular local referencing. For this, relevant keywords related to your industry play an essential role in generating conversions. However, does this visibility strategy really only have advantages? What can be the disadvantages for his web project in the long term?

What are the real advantages of natural referencing?

ALL SEO PROFESSIONALS can tell you: Using a natural SEO strategy is an excellent thing to land in the natural results of a Google search. It allows first and foremost to improve its positioning on the net, in a sustainable way. Indeed, you can capitalize on the actions of organic referencing of the pages of your site, in order to reinforce their visibility in the long term. In addition, SEO has a multi-support dimension between different search engines such as Google, Bing, Yahoo, Ask and others.

In addition to appearing in the first results of search engines, natural referencing allows you to concretely position your site , in a sustainable and profitable way in the long term. The global referencing in e-marketing will allow you to enjoy a very interesting return on investment, while allowing you to be visible. The E-reputation of your company was also improved, even without the preparation of a colossal budget for paid referencing or a particular referencing policy.

Improve the positioning of your site in search engine results

UNLIKE PAID REFERENCING, natural referencing allows you to have a good diversified referencing in the search results. In the case of paid referencing, only one position is possible per advertiser. You will gain more traffic and get a much better conversion rate by occupying more places in the natural results of Google.

A gain of more qualified natural traffic

IF YOU ACHIEVE GOOD internet positioning thanks to natural referencing, it means that your seo content is really relevant. This will automatically generate qualified and duplicate traffic. The SEO of sites is not only about money, but also about quality content. You will more easily get clicks from incoming links thanks to local natural referencing. It is probably best to entrust the creation of your website to a well-structured professional for optimal natural referencing.

The positioning of a site is free thanks to natural referencing

AMONG THE MOST USED referencing techniques in order to improve the site's referencing, seo natural referencing remains one of the most popular. The root cause is that you can do SEO for free. Then, if you want to use a natural referencing agency, it will be another story on the invoice side. In any case, you can do seo training yourself and embark on the adventure for free. Note that a paid SEO service can cost you up to €7 per click for certain sectors such as law or finance. Working on SEO and all Seo sem techniques will never have seemed so essential!

What are the disadvantages of implementing an SEO strategy?

IF YOUR GOAL IS TO improve Google referencing and gain notoriety over the long term, referencing sites in seo optimization will be useful to you. On the other hand, if you are in a hurry to generate traffic and therefore results and profit, the long tail delay of natural referencing may seem burdensome to you. Indeed, seo optimization can take several weeks or months before bearing fruit.

SEO is not a short-term solution

FOR WEB REFERENCING to work perfectly, each page will have to undergo indexing and optimization. To position your site from the start, it may be wise to use an SEO guide, but also to call on a webmarketing agency. This seo referencing agency can provide you with answers to your questions and suggest that you set up a more suitable visibility strategy. Perhaps – why not – by mixing effective natural referencing and paid referencing. For traffic acquisition, the redesign of poorly optimized sites will first go through an seo audit, then through a paid referencing campaign, before stabilizing with long-term natural referencing

CONCLUSION

IN CONCLUSION, SEO is a powerful and essential tool for any website looking to increase its visibility and drive more traffic. By understanding the various elements of SEO and implementing the strategies outlined in this book, you'll be well on your way to climbing the search engine rankings and reaching more people with your website.

We've covered everything from keyword research to link building, from on-page optimization to technical SEO, and from content creation to social media. By following the tips and tricks outlined in this book, you'll be able to optimize your website for maximum visibility and performance.

It's important to note that SEO is an ongoing process, and you should be constantly monitoring and adjusting your strategies to stay ahead of the curve. Regularly check your website's analytics and keep an eye on the latest trends and best practices in SEO. The search engine algorithms and ranking factors are always changing, so it's essential to stay up-to-date with the latest techniques and strategies.

We hope that this book has been helpful in guiding you through the process of optimizing your website for search engines. Remember that SEO is a marathon, not a sprint and it takes time, patience and persistence to see the results. Keep learning and experimenting, and you'll be sure to see your website climbing the search engine rankings in no time!

Don't miss out!

Visit the website below and you can sign up to receive emails whenever RC PRABIR publishes a new book. There's no charge and no obligation.

https://books2read.com/r/B-A-AAWFB-UNRIF

BOOKS 2 READ

Connecting independent readers to independent writers.

Did you love *What is SEO? A Comprehensive Guide for Beginners*? Then you should read *Real Ways To Make Money From Home : Proven Offline and Online Strategies for Financial Success*[1] by RC PRABIR!

[2]

Unlock the secrets to making money quickly with real, proven methods that actually work. This book dives into practical strategies and actionable steps designed to help you boost your income in record time. From leveraging online opportunities to smart side hustles and creative approaches to earning, every chapter is packed with insights that are easy to implement. Whether you're looking to tackle financial challenges or simply want to increase your cash flow, this guide offers the tools and tips to make it happen efficiently and effectively. Perfect for anyone seeking fast, reliable ways to achieve financial success.

---

1. https://books2read.com/u/4AldNK
2. https://books2read.com/u/4AldNK

Also by RC PRABIR

DIY House Hacks
DIY House Hacks: Clever Fixes for Modern Living

Standalone
Real Ways To Make Money From Home : Proven Offline and Online Strategies for Financial Success
What is SEO? A Comprehensive Guide for Beginners

www.ingramcontent.com/pod-product-compliance
Lightning Source LLC
LaVergne TN
LVHW022050200926
848481LV00003B/853